THE GLASG
&

RESTAURANT
GUIDE

by

Sandra Wilson, Sheila Adamson
& Allan Hutcheon.

£3.45

A Guide to Over 100 Pubs & Restaurants

POLYGON BOOKS

First published by
Polygon
22 George Square, Edinburgh

Printed in Great Britain by
Bell & Bain Ltd
Glasgow

British Library Cataloguing
in Publication Data
Wilson, Sandra
The Glasgow pub and restaurant guide.
1. Scotland. Strathclyde Region. Glasgow.
Public houses—Visitors guides
2. Scotland. Restaurant
I. Title II. Adamson, Sheila III. Hutcheon, Allan
647.'9541443

ISBN 0 948275 57 X

THE GLASGOW PUB & RESTAURANT GUIDE

Authors: Sandra Wilson, Sheila Adamson, Allan Hutcheon.

Hingers On: Robin Taggart, Mikey McCormick, Owen, Neil, Phil Armes & Pat Urquhart.

Cover Illustration By: Rosamund Fowler
Photography By: Paula Carley
Additional Photographs By: Sandra Wilson
Maps & Symbols by: Janice Taylor

Typeset & Designed on Apricot Computer by:
Sandra Wilson & Sheila Adamson.

Special Thanks To: The library assistants at the Mitchell Library.

Real Ale

Meals

Puggy Machines

Live Music

T.V.

Condom Machine

Sunday Opening

TRON *EFFECTIVE DIRECT* MARKETING

THE GLASGOW

The oldest industry in Glasow is the brewing of beer. It is believed to have been started by the monks in the days of St Mungo. The firm of John & Robert Tennent, Brewers existed in 1556. Beer is still brewed approximately on the same site where the monks operated. Glasgow's culture and history is steeped in and sometimes strongly associated with drinking. In Glasgow today there are over 650 public houses, many of them supplied by Tennent Caledonian Breweries. While Tennents have a strong hold on the city, Alloas & Whitbreads are beginning to make their mark. CAMRA, the Campaign for Real Ale has revived the interest in Real Ale in Glasgow, producing their own CAMRA guide to real ale pubs in the West of Scotland. Although the West based Strathalbyn Brewery has recently gone bust, you can still get a good pint of Belhaven Bill, Greenmantle or Maclay's.

Since publication of the last Polygon Glasgow Pub Guide (1983) the range and variety of howffs has changed dramatically. Foreign & imported beers such as Furstenberg, Beck's, Red Stripe etc. are now widely available. There has also been a rapid increase in the number of French style Cafe/ Bistros such as Nico's & Cafe Noir. This dramatic change in drinking habits has necessitated a completely updated and revised edition of the Glasgow Pub Guide.

In many areas the public house is the last remnant of a broken community, which has made way for new housing and commercial developments. For example in the Gorbals. The new breed have ventured into parts of the city centre currently being rejuvenated. The Merchant city is a stunning example of a Central Government and District Council initiative to revitalise this once derelict area, destroying Glasgow's image of 'No Mean City'. Lately Glasgow has been sponsor and promoter of events such as the Garden Festival '88, attracting a great deal of attention at home and abroad. The city recently won the honour of European City of Culture 1990, robbing its more sophisticated neighbour Edinburgh of the award. While these improvements in the city have given Glaswegians a new pride in their town, they have also heightened the divide between the "haves" and "have nots"!

Glasgow is a strong working class city, and as such going out to the pub is still an occasion to dress up for. The last bastion of working men's pubs like the Corona Bar in Shawlands or the Saracen Head in Gallowgate are fading fast, facing take over by the new concept and fashion bars. While it is sad to see these establishments disappearing, they are also taking with them attitudes of sexism. Women are now fully accepted in pubs, the last to open its doors to women being Glasgow University Student Union, although still known as the "Men's Union"!

Glasgow's history is full of character and characters, much of which has a connection with drink and drinking. For this reason, we have headed each page of this guide with interesting, fascinating, and sometimes useless, facts about bingeing and bevvying in this fair city.

In selecting over 100 pubs and restaurants we have tried to cover a broad range & variety. Each of the four main areas of the guide, City Centre, Merchant City, West End and South Side all have their own distinctive and different character & atmosphere. The West, historically prosperous, end of the city has a large student and media type population. The once temperance dry South Side has a high proportion of fun bars, with an emphasis on theme evenings. The Merchant City pubs are perhaps unfairly branded with the Yuppie, Dinky image. I say perhaps unfairly because the majority of pubs like Babbity Bowster strive hard to attract a broad cross section of people, from all income brackets.

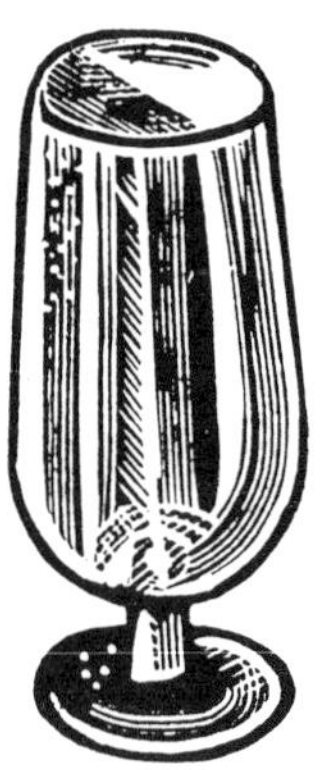

New pubs are trying harder and harder to compete and hang on to your custom, even to the extent of creating and operating a strict door policy to attract a particular type of clientele, for example in the Mission in Battlefield. It cannot be long before several of the pubs reviewed here lose the fight. Many of the new hostelries are now combining a restaurant and bar, tempting drinkers in, with the offer of serving snacks and meals at most hours of the day or night. Witness the Baby Grand at Charing Cross who are

now open until 5am on Friday/Saturday evenings, serving meals and soft drinks after midnight. Perhaps we just feel the need to keep ahead of our English cousins who have just had their licensing hours improved to match our own, or perhaps we are witnessing the dawn of a new style of eating and drinking, with many more to follow this example.

Eating houses have also seen an improvement in the quality & variety of culinary fayre, a dramatic change in eating habits since the days of "Annacker's Midden"! An upsurge in continental food, salad and seafood, one or two new places offering New Orleans Cajun style eating, but still dominated by the Chilli, Burgers, Pizza variety. Gentrification of Glasgow has also seen a growth in overpriced establishments. Whatever your taste or pocket, Glasgow is bound to have a restaurant to accommodate you.

In some instances it has been difficult to make a sharp distinction between pubs and restaurants, however we have tried and have separated the guide into two. THE GLASGOW PUB GUIDE on one side, flipping over to find THE GLASGOW RESTAURANT GUIDE on the other. There are maps to the four main areas, & symbols denote facilities offered, allowing you to plan & choose your evening of food and drink carefully, thereby ensuring a good night if you are new to the city.

While all the reviews are obviously biased & subjective, they are hopefully not without justification, enabling you to recognise that while we praise a pub for its basic down to earth qualities, if you are looking for a fun, loud disco type bar, then this particular establishment is unlikely to appeal!

The guide is intended for Glaswegian natives, new Glaswegians and it should prove invaluable to the vast influx of visitors from home and abroad. Guid health!

THE GLASGOW

CONTENTS

PUBS

PUBLISHER'S NOTE: Details published in this guide concerning prices of food & drinks were correct to the best of our knowledge at the time of going to press. Information about opening hours may also be subject to change as applications for extended licences were being made towards the end of September, '88.

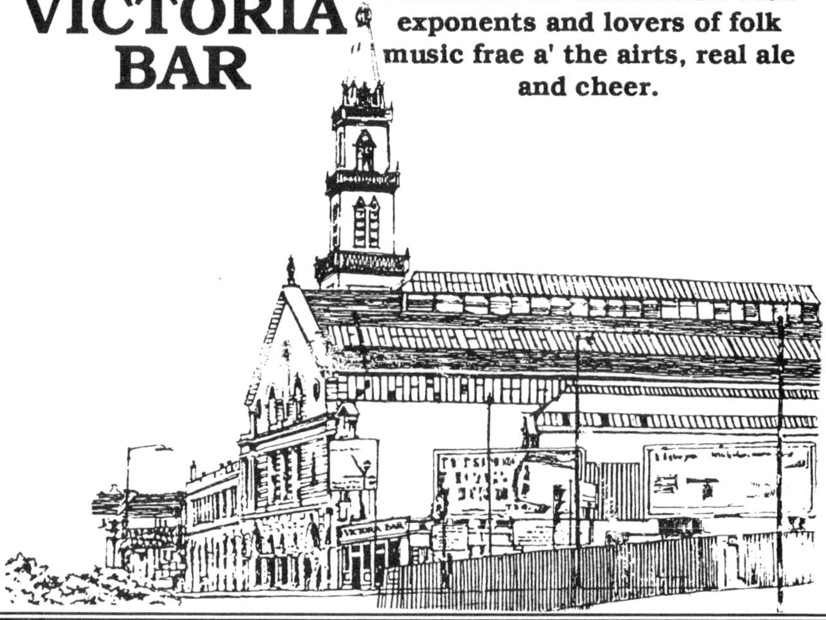

THE GLASGOW

1. ADVOCATE
2. ATHOLL ARMS
3. BABY GRAND
4. BAR LUXEMBOURG
5. BON ACCORD
6. BRAHMS & LISZT
7. CAFE NOIR
8. CARNEGIES BAR/DINER
9. CHARLIE PARKERS
10. CORN EXCHANGE
11. DE QUINCEYS
12. FOUQUETS BAR/DINER
13. GRIFFIN
14. HOOTERS
15. HORSESHOE BAR
16. INTERMEZZO CAFE/BAR
17. LA TANIERE
18. LAUDERS
19. L'ODEON CAFE BAR
20. MALTMAN
21. NEW CHANCERY
22. NICO'S
23. NILE CAFE/BAR
24. O'HENRYS CAFE/BAR
25. PELICAN BLONDE
26. POT STILL
27. PYTHAGORAS
28. RITZ
29. ROCK GARDEN
30. ROTUNDA (NORTH)
31. SCARAMOUCHE
32. SHENANIGANS
33. SLOAN'S
34. SMITHS WINE BAR
35. 39 STEPS
36. TIMES SQUARE

RESTAURANTS

37. BALBIR'S ASHOKA TANDOORI
38. BUTTERY
39. CHANGE AT JAMAICA
40. HANRAHANS
41. JUST NUTS CAFE/DINER
42. KOH - I - NOOR
43. NEW FAR EAST
44. PUMP HOUSE
45. RAMANA
46. ROGANO
47. TRADING POST
48. VICEROY

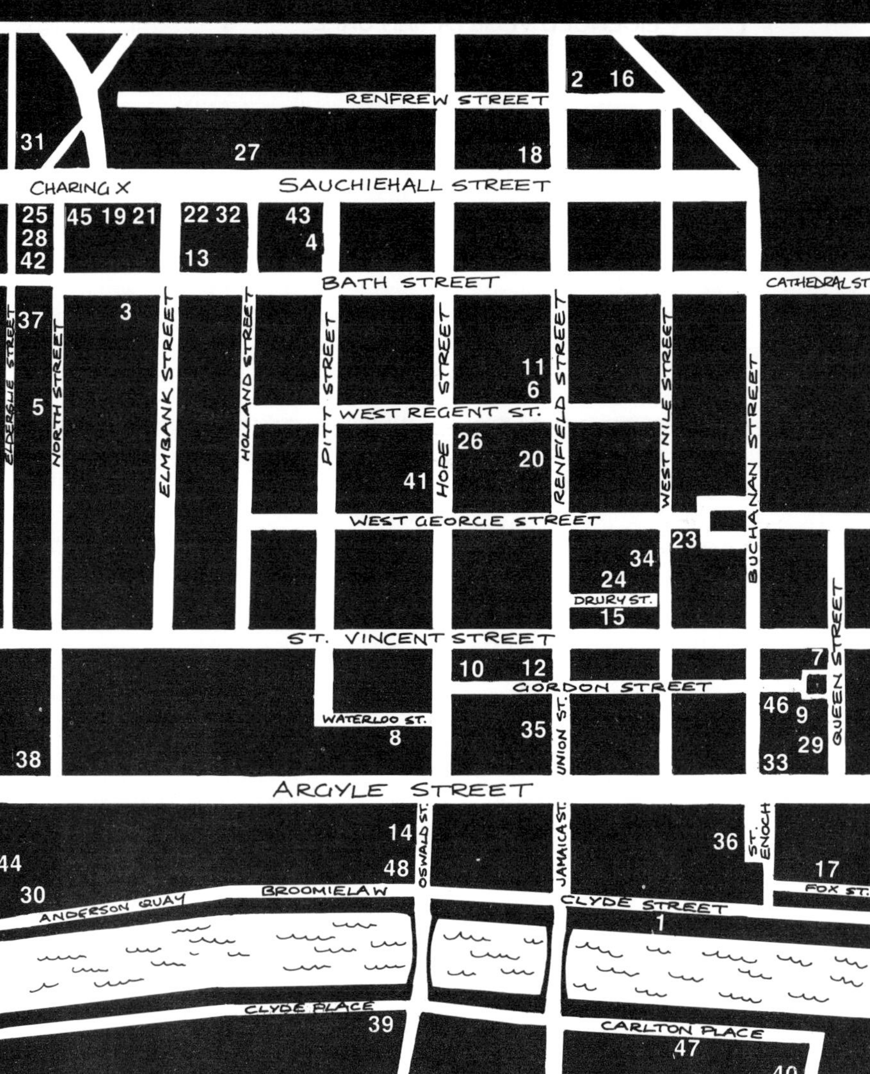

PUB GUIDE

IN 1853 WHEN GLASGOW HAD A POPULATION OF OVER 350,000 THERE WAS A PUBLIC HOUSE FOR EVERY 130 PEOPLE.

ADVOCATE

Customs House Quay Gardens

TEL: 221 0021

Foster's, Budweiser.

Opened in '83, the Advocate was alone amongst the new breed of pubs to recognise the advantages of locating on the waterfront. Known then as the Devil's Advocate, it preceded the now famous Glasgow Sheriff Court, on the opposite bank. The Court is renowned as the largest in Europe. Although the Devil has departed from the Advocate, it retains strong judiciary connections. The clockwork judge, whose liver must be in ruins, systematically pours claret down his throat, from his permanent position at the "Bar", confirming a commonly held opinion of those who sit in judgement.

The rich decor, leather chesterfields, open fire and antique fireplace typify the quiet daytime atmosphere, when custom is largely made up of the business community. A much younger, livelier clientage emerges in the evening, no doubt drawn by the adjacent disco, Panama Jax. Food is available during the day, ranging from light snacks to substantial, reasonably priced meals, but the major summer attraction of the Advocate is the facility to eat and drink outdoors, with a magnificent view of the River Clyde.

At the time of going to press, work has begun extending and refurbishing the premises. The exciting focal point of the design being a glass domed structure which will overhang the walkway. I am hopeful that the existing atmosphere of the Advocate will not be lost with this imaginative new project, and given the owner's proven ability to accurately "judge" what people want, my concern will probably be "NOT PROVEN".

ATHOLL ARMS

134 Renfrew/Renfield Street

TEL: 332 5265

Tartan Special, McEwan's 80/-, Beck's.

Once a real spit and sawdust bar, the Atholl Arms has been refurbished both inside and out. Designed and managed by David Anderson (of Baby Grand/Blue Note Fame!) the new decor is a tasteful mix of wood panelled walls, var-

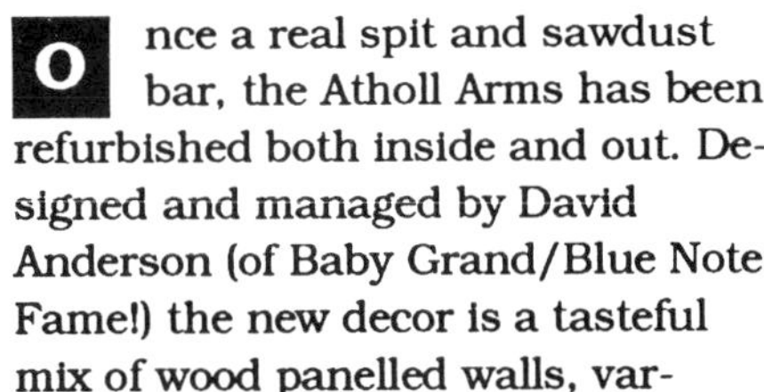

nished floors, and green flourishing plants. On the corner of Renfrew and Renfield Street, the bar has a fresh, light & airy atmosphere, aided by small bottles of fresh carnations on each of the 20 or so tables.

Close to Scottish Television studios and across from the Pavilion Theatre, the clientele consists of mainly media and theatre types and the odd culture vulture.

Becks beer on draught is an attraction, as is the bottled Grolsh, Furstenberg and Budweiser, and the price range is what you would expect from the city centre.

Also on offer are reasonably priced meals at lunchtimes, ideal for the business lunch, and bar snacks in the evenings. Jazz and rhythm & blues music in the background complement this attractive and pleasant pub.

BABY GRAND

3/7 Elmbank Gardens

TEL: 248 4942

McEwan's 80/-, Beck's.

The Baby Grand is an interesting pub/cafe situated across from Charing Cross train station. It looks strangely out of place amongst towering office blocks within an off street complex. It is very small and has the buzz of a smart but casual, continental cafe. The usual range of beers and lagers, complemented by foreign brands on draught are available to the clientele, which tends to be within the 21 to 35 age group.

The food is unusual , for example, Italian Sausage with Lentils, or Smoked Venison on Pumpernickel Bread and New York Pastrami are hardly likely to be seen elsewhere! The unusual menu does not come cheaply, nor do the drinks, but it is unusual.

As the name suggests, there is a baby grand piano on the premises, although the live music which was a feature no longer is. Definitely a pub for those of you who have "a few bob", and there must be quite a number of people in this category as the place gets extremely busy.

BAR LUXEMBOURG

197 Pitt Street

TEL: 332 1111

Alloa 70/-, XXXX, Lowenbrau.

The crypt of one of Glasgow's old churches now converted. Transformed, the crypt now houses a terraced dining area. Predominantly white decor with unusual white ceiling drapes creating a very light, continental atmosphere. A feature is the Conifer tree in what used to be a fountain!

Clientele is predominately young and at the weekends the bar is wall to wall fashion. Music is exclusively current chart sounds and loud! A large video screen over the bar shows pop videos with no sound - it doesn't seem to add anything to the atmosphere but everyone seems to watch the screen nevertheless.

An excellent selection of fifteen european & continental bottled beers is available.

Meals are available at lunchtimes and in the evenings. Soup, Prawn & Mussels starters, Pizzas, Pasta and Salad at prices to suit all pockets. A popular main course includes Chargrilled Sirloin Steak, finished off with either caramel shortcake or Banana Split.

Below Cardinal Follies Discoteque , this is a good warm up station,before dancing the night away!

BON ACCORD

153 North Street

TEL: 248 4427

Real Ale experts abound in this infamous pub. Often the banter across the bar could be mistaken for a Mastermind warm-up session, speciality subject - beer.

Only brave men ask for lager! - a notice above the bar courteously warns new customers of the dangers that such a request could present. Apart from the "ale-drinking caricatures" you will find a real mix of customers here, some carrying indefinable musical instruments, some the Financial Times and others sporting motorbike mags or "The Punter's Guide to Beating the Bookie at his own Game". Few women frequent the Bon Accord - but those who do are definitely "new, independent women". Food is available and although positively unstartling, the menu exhibits the same "live and let live" atmosphere which prevails.

A refreshing, interesting bar that has an abundance of character, and of course, beer, with in excess of 16 beers either on tap or hand-pumped. They do give gantry space to spirits, the very odd wine and even lager, so don't feel obliged to borrow a Beer Encyclopedia or join CAMRA - no one will mind, really.

BRAHMS & LISZT

71 Renfield Street

TEL: 333 0633

Castle Eden, Heineken, Stella.

Well known for selling ale by the jug, this city centre hostelry now also sells spirits, having eventually succumbed to the demand. It is equally well known for its large barrels of peanuts which customers can help themselves to. The traditional sawdust is replaced by peanut shells. Tables are candlelit and the shelved walls are covered in old paintings, photographs and bric a brac. A pub where one can spend hours studying the walls and inscriptions around the dark wooden bar, it's nooks and crannies. A mellow atmosphere aided by the mood music which is mainly rhythm & blues and jazz. Popular with students and leather-clad bikers.

Healthy wholesome pub grub, such as Beef & Guinness Pie and Ploughmans Lunches can be washed down with a glass of wine from their extensive cellars, in this unusual basement pub.

CAFE NOIR

BRASSERIE & BISTRO
151 Queen Street

TEL: 248 3525

Campbell's 70/-, Heineken, Stella.

When Cafe Noir first opened in '83, Glaswegians were very pleasantly surprised at the standard of decor, with sofas, decorative wrought iron work and luxurious wood. Many have since used the same design idea, but the cafe has continued to have a successful "individual" style which is very comfortable.

Food is available all day. Breakfast is served from 8.30 am; a salad bar menu between 5 and 8 pm; salad bar from noon till 6pm as well as a full menu in the downstairs restaurant. So whether you want a hot Croissant, Crepes, Steak, vegetarian food or Chocolate and Drambuie Mousse, Cafe Noir can provide! Although there are strong French influences, the menu should be described as "international" as dishes from far and wide are available.

This Brasserie and Bistro manages to be very relaxed and comfortable during the day, however, if you're looking for a quiet venue in the evening go elsewhere, as the bar buzzes with activity, especially between Wednesdays and Sundays, when it is standing room only!

A pianist performs downstairs and it's one of too few places where you can take your children, outwith licensing hours. A well established, popular place to eat, drink, relax with the daily newspapers or have a fun night out.

THE GLASGOW

CARNEGIE'S BAR/ DINER

21 Waterloo Street

TEL: 221 4231

Tartan Special, McEwan's 80/-.

Carnegie's custom is mainly drawn from local offices and businesses, being well placed opposite Central Station. The main bar is fairly non descript - dark green walls, plastic greenery brightened up by full length dusty pink festoon blinds, complete with black & white photographs of bodies in various states of undress - both male & female. Waitress service is available to save you from squeezing through to the bar as it can get quite busy in the evenings.

The downstairs bar has a more tropical feel, with a resident D.J. seven nights a week attracting quite a crowd.

Sharing a menu with Fouquets - they are owned by the same people - a wide selection of dishes is available, from Norwegian Prawn Cocktail, several vegetarian dishes and a good variety of steaks & specially prepared sauces to match.

Not a bad wee place for the occasional drink!

CHARLIE PARKERS

21 Royal Exchange Square

TEL: 248 3040

Alloa Heavy, Lowenbrau, Skol.

Reputed to be a classy establishment and highly praised in the last Glasgow Pub Guide ('83), I looked forward to updating a review for this issue. Regrettably, their past efficiency has lapsed to such a degree that I failed on four separate visits to secure their "efficient services". Had I been offering anything other than an opportunity to comment on my draft review, I could understand their lack of courtesy. Elitism is not a new phenomenon in Charlie Parkers. When first opened it attracted the attention of the licensing authorities and the media, who obviously felt compelled to investigate a volume of complaints from members of the public, whose faces it seems, did not fit. Certainly in those heady days which saw the birth of a new style of pub, Charlie Parkers was both outrageous and entertaining. Customers tended to wear colourful "over the top" ballroom dresses, whilst sipping blue or green drinks. Personally, I liked the colour and the sense of fun, although the careful "screening" of potential customers attempting to gain entry cannot be condoned!

Still a favourite haunt of the more affluent drinker, you might want to visit Charlie Parkers to partake in a little voyeurism, or simply to find out if YOUR face fits!

Charlie Parkers offer a special "party kit" which promises that your meal will be cooked and served by unemployed actors and actresses. I hadn't realised that the acting profession and culinary proficiency were synonymous. Well, at least they'll be familiar with bad reviews!

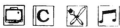

CORN EXCHANGE

88 Gordon Street

TEL: 248 5380

Dryborough's 70/-, Alloa 80/-, Skol, XXXX, Lowenbrau.

irectly opposite Central Station this small cosy bar does well from the passing trade of thirsty travellers and business people on their way to make another deal, or perhaps making it in the Corn Exchange. Although only opened in early '88, the bar looks as if it has been established for 40 years, furnished with wrought iron tables and comfortable seating. Very reasonable traditional lunchtime fayre is offered in the back room, or downstairs, between 11am and 3pm. You can even have a game of cards or cribbage borrowed from behind the bar while you wait to catch your train. A smart compact wee pub.

DE QUINCEY'S

71 Renfield Street

TEL: 333 9725

Castle Eden, Moosehead, Stella, Heineken.

This list of beers suggests a down to earth pub, but there is an positively elegant atmosphere about this city centre wine bar, reminiscent of colonial times. Dequincey's was originally an insurance office, and it was only after it had been purchased that the original wall tiles were uncovered. The tiles are quite exquisite, scallop shapes encompassing high pillars, ceiling and walls. Broken tiles have a high insurance value as replacements have to be hand-made. The opulent aura is further enhanced by the venetian glass chandeliers, leather couches, white rafia cane chairs and festoon blinds.

Carvery/buffet meals are available all day ranging from a generous helping of Roast Beef to Seafood Escalopes as well as a range of salads and some tempting fresh cream gateau. A little more expensive than your average pub lunch, but worth it to soak up the atmosphere. A good range of French and German wines is also on offer.

Across from the Odeon cinema, the clientele is from all walks of life, lawyers, engineers and cinema usherettes can be found rubbing shoulders.

FOUQUET'S BAR/ DINER

7 Renfield Street

TEL: 226 4958

Heineken, Stella.

I recall the opening of Fouquet's. Along with some work colleagues we decided to celebrate an event, now long since forgotten, in this new diner. It was spacious, well designed and "awfy posh". We enjoyed lunch and indulged in a few more of the "free whisky promotion samples" than was wise at midday. On returning recently, my mental image was shaken to such a degree that I returned upstairs to the door to check if my automatic navigation had let me down. It hadn't, but Fouquet's has changed. Still spacious, still the same design and no longer "awfy posh", it has become a favourite haunt of the young, gregarious, energetic, "game for anything" crowd. A place for the live-wires, or, like me, those who just watch the live-wires sparking! A bar that runs a happy hour - but most hours seem pretty happy anyway.

Resident D.J., 60's and 70's nights and special events regularly feature. I think the volume could be overwhelming, but I accept that this might be a minority view as no-one else showed any signs of discomfort.

The separate Dining area offers an extensive menu between 12 noon and 10.30 pm. Specialising in steaks which are excellent value, eg a 12oz Club Steak for less than £5, the menu combines some very unusual dishes - try the Vegetable Stroganoff with cream and brandy sauce or the Steak Baguette with salad, both well under £3. If you have a sweet tooth, or you use up a lot of energy, the Toffee/Vanilla/ Coffee Ice Cream with Butterscotch Sauce and whipped cream should fuel a few hours of dancing.

If seeking a pretty wild night out, the atmosphere of Fouquet's should ensure that you achieve it. "The price is right" so don't hesitate at the front door - "Come on Down!"

GRIFFIN

266 Bath Street

TEL: 332 2391

Tennent's Beers.

A famous Glasgow institution and a popular haunt over the years for students, punks, buskers and the occasional French tourist. All of this and a healthy sprinkling of local characters too! The Griffin comprises three bars. There are the main public bar and two satellite lounges, namely the Griffinette & the Griffiny. The bar is a strange mix of the traditional and sixties' kitsch with its solid wooden bar, etched windows (which used to be crystal), plastic bunting and even more plastic orange lampshades. The overall effect is snug and warm, reminiscent somehow of the bar on the Western Isles Ferry - and that's before you've had a few drinks. Prices are very reasonable and the service is fast and efficient. Snax & lunches are served daily from 11am - 7 pm. If you are "bohemian" and have a leather jacket, this could be the place for you.

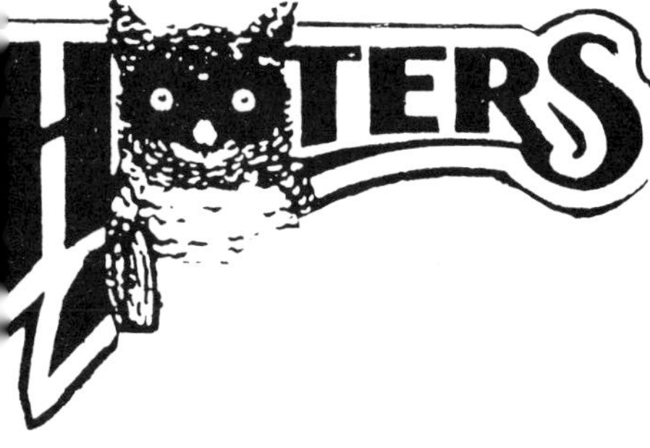

HOOTERS

15/29 Oswald Street

TEL: 221 4583

Tennent's beers.

A large American memorabilia bar and restaurant. A beautiful Juke Box, which looks like an original and it works, sits at one end of the bar beneath photographs of John Wayne and American cartoon strips. Continuing this theme, flags of the States are draped from the ceiling. Hosting regular promotion evenings for Pernod, Schlitz et al at silly prices, happy hours operate between 9pm and midnight on Saturday and Sunday evenings attracting quite a crowd. A pine bar with several raised gallery areas, alcoves, pine tables, chairs and plenty of standing room - not a pub to pine away the lonely hours!

A spot to make a beeline for is "Hoot's Hut", a small compact wooden retreat for those who don't want to be in the spotlight. Stained glass owls are the main reference to our feathered friends in this barn of a place.

Food is available all day, meals being served between noon and 3pm. Carrying a good selection of American and foreign bottled and canned beers/lagers alongside cocktails and a Wine of the Week. It can be fairly quiet midweek, but a lively young crowd who are out to enjoy themselves at the weekend dominate.

HORSESHOE BAR

17 - 21 Drury Street

TEL: 221 3051

Tennent's Beers, Heriot 80/-, Greenmantle, Maclay's.

Established over 100 years ago, the Horseshoe has the longest continuous bar in the United Kingdom according to the Guinness Book of Records '88. This large bar is well staffed, 14 staff at weekends and doormen. Boasting the biggest turnover in lager in the Tennent's group, the cellar holds 6 x 180 gallon tanks, 4 of lager, 2 of heavy, on a good Friday night a tank of lager is easily emptied. The original owner of the bar John Y. Whyte's initials are to be found everywhere, engraved in brass, wood and stone. A magnificently well preserved Victorian bar, etched glass & mirrors, carved wooden wall panelling create a very traditional atmosphere, in both bars upstairs and down. However, the upstairs Horseshoe shaped bar has been removed to create more space for the young disco crowd.

Popular at all times of the week, the bar is frequented by a varied crowd of businessmen, railwaymen from nearby Central Station and good socialists no doubt attracted by the real ale. Another attraction has to be the reasonably priced meals at lunchtimes. A three course lunch, home made soup, Steak Pie, Rice & Fruit Pudding is served up by friendly courteous and quick waitresses, either at the bar or the table if you prefer. A good thriving, bustling city-centre pub in the traditional style.

INTERMEZZO

A little off the main drag, this bar strives to do well with friendly service. Habitues are media/arty types and lovers of traditional Scottish fayre.

INTERMEZZO CAFE/ BAR

22 Renfrew Street

TEL: 332 6288

Tennent's Beers, Maclay's.

In keeping, this stylish cafe/ bar has large black & white stills of Ingrid Bergman & Leslie Howard from the movie of the same name. The owners have made good use of the small space & high ceiling by building a gallery floor overlooking the bar and incorporating three ceiling-high art deco mirrors. The bar is furnished with art deco stained glass wall lights & pastel lilac & green wall coverings creating a warm glowing ambience.

Open from 8am, a breakfast menu is available, choose from your basic bacon buttie & scrambled eggs to the full gourmet breakfast - smoked salmon, eggs, wholemeal toast & freshly squeezed orange juice & coffee.

The traditional Scottish dishes on the menu at lunchtimes are one of the main reasons why you should visit this establishment. Loch Fyne Smoked Salmon, Marinated Herring & Haddock Pie are all very reasonably priced. Food is available all day until 8pm.

LA TANIERE

15 Fox Street

TEL: 221 4844

Dryborough's, Alloa 70/-, XXXX, Skol, Lowenbrau, Arrol's.

Converted from an old ware house, La Taniere is a little out of the way, but worth seeking out. A small pub with a balcony holding five tables, which face not too flattering, life-size models of Ronnie Reagan and Margaret Thatcher.

Very quiet at lunchtimes, although the Italian and Scottish home made grub is good value for money.

Despite it's small size, La Taniere provides live entertainment every night of the week and Saturday afternoons. If the weather's good, the bands play outside on the patio. The bands are young and local and play all types of music.

Archibald Arrol's real ale is an attraction as is the Magnum of Henrell Trocken Champagne, or so we're told! A mixed crowd that varies from night to night depending on the band. Very popular at weekends.

LAUDER'S

Sauchiehall Street/Renfield Street

TEL: 332 9478

Tennent's Beers.

This established bar does well from the passing trade of shoppers from Sauchiehall Street during the day and Pavilion Theatre goers in the evenings. It has also built up a reputation for being one of the best singles bars in town.

Named after Harry Lauder, famous Scots singer/comedian, there is a strong music hall atmosphere about this bar. Walls are covered with original Pavilion programmes & other theatrical memorabilia. Dark red chesterfield couches dominate one end of the bar and comfortable tables & chairs the other, next to the deservedly popular grill/diner.

A classic Wurlitzer juke box has pride of place in the bar, loaded with classic sixties sounds, which pleases the weekend clientele, many of whom are mature enough to remember when the songs were first released. On a good Friday evening you can join in a real sing-a-long! Ceiling fans help circulate the air of the bar in the evenings but particularly at weekends when it is mobbed.

The clientele depends what's on at the Pavilion, you can never really be sure what to expect!

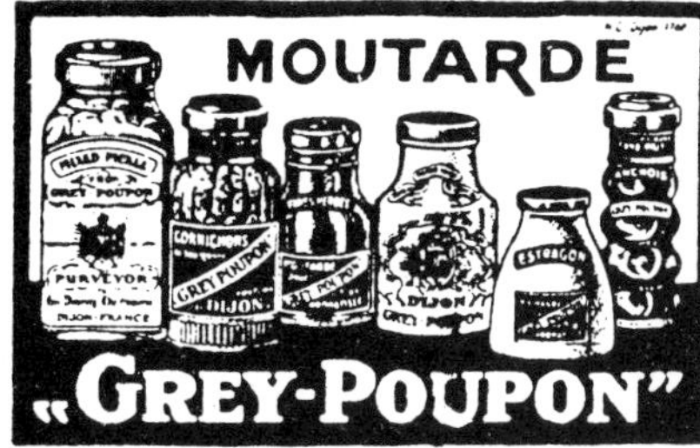

L'ODEON CAFE/BAR

427/431 Sauchiehall Street

TEL: 332 3141

Campbell's 70/-, Stella, Heineken, Moosehead.

This site has been striving for an identity for several years now, previously known as the Dome and Centre Court- famous for being one of the earliest known theme pubs in the city. Now doing well as a parisienne cafe bar, tastefully decorated with dark wood panelling, an impressive extended Victorian Gantry incorporating large boxed wine racks either side & flourishing greenery.

The designers have captured a clean comfortable atmosphere, with varnished floors, tortoiseshell framed French posters and glass & linen topped tables. The bar has a bright airy feel to it during the day. Ludo, Trivial Pursuits & other games are available from behind the bar, as are the day's newspapers. An upright piano stands in one corner, although I doubt if it's ever played.

Meals and snacks are available at the rear of the bar, concentrating on Crepes, all of which are freshly made using a L'Odeon wholemeal recipe. Continental style breakfast is available till noon each day.

Poaching some long established trade from Nico's, a drink here beats a night at the pictures!

THE MALTMAN

61 Renfield Street

TEL: 332 0717

McEwan's 80/-, Tennent's 70/-, Beck's, Greenmantle.

The Maltman houses three separate bars, the Vines, Coffey's house and the first no smoking bar in Scotland. As you would expect , it has a wide range of over 100 single malt whiskies! Coffey's house is named after Aeneas Coffey who was at one time Inspector General Excise for Ireland, who in 1830 invented a superior patent Still for the creation of grain whisky. On the whole the decor of the bars gives this pub no real atmosphere and the whisky theme is not fully realised. The range of whiskies apart, plastic vines, grubby floor covering and small booths result in a style that's not very much of anything. However some live jazz sessions on Saturday evenings are popular.

Connoisseurs of malts will obviously be motivated to use this pub, but a facelift and a stronger identity would not go amiss!

NEW CHANCERY

421 Sauchiehall Street

TEL: 333 9026

Tennent's Beers, Beck's.

Ideally situated amongst a diverse selection of bars in Sauchiehall Street, the New Chancery offers a different atmosphere to that of neighbouring bars. Aspiring to the classy, trendy level of its neighbours, L'Odeon and Nico's, it falls between these and Pythagoras, managing to escape the latter's "teeny-bopper" image.

The upstairs restaurant is pricey, but you can enjoy a wide variety of fish, poultry and other equally inviting cuisine. The ground floor lounge is my preferred option with Beck's and Carlsberg on draught at very good prices. The bar lunches are also well priced. With live music on offer four nights a week, it is not what you might describe as dull!

NICO'S

375 Sauchiehall Street

TEL: 332 1585/5736

Tennent's Beers.

If you want to "share" an evening with some of Glasgow's more "bohemian" pub goers, Nico's is the place to be!

I say "share" an evening quite deliberately, as Nico's is the kind of pub where you are quite likely to find yourself joining in the spontaneous entertainment. Be prepared to find yourself listening in to a huddle of serious politics - a good Beatles song comes over the house P.A. - and the huddle suddenly becomes a pub "choir".

It is not uncommon for advertising executives in smart crombie coats to attempt breakdancing late on a Friday night, for art school punks to play chess silently on a Sunday afternoon, or for a man with a dog called Patch to ask you what you think of the situation in Northern Tibet.

If in the right mood, dancing on the bar and very rude jokes are tolerated by the management - as long as you keep on buying rounds of drinks.

The decor of the bar is of a "well lived in" French cafe. A good range of foreign lagers are particularly pleasing to the palate. A feature of this watering hole is the excellent lunch fayre. Vegetarian dishes and fresh salads are most popular, and

WILLIAM HARLEY BUILT A RESERVOIR IN WEST NILE STREET IN 1804. A STOUFUL OF FRESH WATER COST 1D.

are good value for money.

Melodic Jazz is performed live on Sunday lunchtimes, and the ground coffee and hot chocolate are excellent.

NILE CAFE/BAR

58 West Nile Street

TEL: 248 6830

Campbell's 70/-, Heineken, Stella.

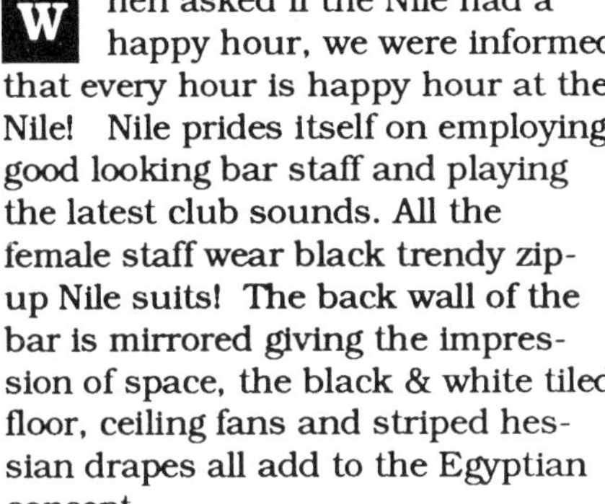

When asked if the Nile had a happy hour, we were informed that every hour is happy hour at the Nile! Nile prides itself on employing good looking bar staff and playing the latest club sounds. All the female staff wear black trendy zip-up Nile suits! The back wall of the bar is mirrored giving the impression of space, the black & white tiled floor, ceiling fans and striped hessian drapes all add to the Egyptian concept.

On the evening we were there, well known eccentric Tory MP Nicholas Fairbairn was in having a few drinks with chums, (he apparently runs a travel shop next door). In the main clientele is made up of office workers from local banks & insurance firms, and we're told that in the evenings when the lights go down the music goes up!

O'HENRY'S CAFE/BAR

14 Drury Street

TEL: 248 3751

Campbell's 70/-, Stella, Heineken.

On three levels, O'Henry's offers characterful surroundings. On entering you will feel the relaxed, welcoming atmosphere, very much associated with more established pubs. A pub frequented by all ages, where the music does not dominate the conversation. A good wine list, served by the bottle or the glass complements the daily, varied seafood menu. Hot chocolate with a generous measure of green Chartreuse merits a mention. Polished wooden floor, rattan & cane tables and chairs are everywhere and whilst these features do not sound extraordinary, the atmosphere and welcome certainly are! It's good to see another establishment that can accommodate your needs at any time of the day or night whether you fancy a snack, cup of coffee or a meal.

A well run pub which should continue to be popular, as it has captured that elusive quality - atmosphere.

PELICAN BLONDE

Sauchiehall Street

Slightly off beat establishment and a bit off the main drag! The decor is bright & jazzy with peach walls, large mirrors and a tiled patterned floor. A place to have a chat or snack on the way into or out of the city centre. An ideal place to meet up with friends before heading out west! A small bistro offering light snacks, such as Pate Shrimps, soup, Pizzas, Lasagne, Baked Potatoes, Croissants and Caramel Shortcake, all reasonably priced. Opened in September '88, they have recently opened downstairs specialising in vegetarian dishes.

Bottled & canned beers include Budweiser, Red Stripe, Grolsh, Becks, Stella & Clausthaler. Earl Grey & China Tea, Expresso & Cappucino are also served. The piped music is mainly black soul & funky. Clientele is young and moody! The type of place where Paul Coia does not look out of place!

POT STILL

154 Hope Street

TEL: 333 0980

Tennent's Beers, Maclay's.

One of a handful of pubs that can boast an impressive selection of malt whiskies - 280 in total, all of which are displayed above and around the bar. We can recommend this pub to all age groups of tourists or Glaswegians looking to broaden their horizons. It is a handy town centre pub, situated half way up Hope Street. Of a comfortable size, with reasonable prices and a friendly, welcoming atmosphere, you could do worse than have a drink here.

The competition in this part of town is pretty stiff and the price of pub lunches surprised me as they are certainly not what you would describe as competitive. Whisky connoisseurs should appreciate the choice and real ale fans will also be pleased, but those who are more interested in pub lunches should look elsewhere.

PYTHAGORAS

410 Sauchiehall Street

TEL: 332 3495

Alloa Beers, Skol, XXXX, Lowenbrau.

They say quantity does not nec essarily mean quality, and this is certainly true in Pythagoras case. With three separate lounge areas and a maximum capacity of around 300, I am stretched to find any aspect which can be illuminated as unique.

Pythagoras claim that their different lounges cater for different clients. There's the restaurant style lounge, where one can sample a moderate breakfast, lunch or evening meal at above moderate costs. There's a second fairly comfortable lounge which, for most of the time, will generally accommodate anyone from the "mine is a pint and a packet of crisps " punter to the "cigar and a glass of Port please " type. Party goers frequent lounge number three, which at weekends, overspills into lounges one and two. At this time the over 21's are advised to leave and search for more mature surroundings.

The manager insisted that we emphasise that they have a selection of six different cans behind the bar (although I'm not sure why?). It obviously holds an appeal for the, dare I say it, "teeny-boppers", and perhaps it is old age which leads me to conclude that I won't become a regular!

THE RITZ

241 North Street

TEL: 226 4419

McEwan's 80/-, Tartan Special, Harp, Beck's.

The Ritz has a wonderful frontage of architectural interest. The problem is that you have to be standing immediately outside to see it as the Ritz is hidden from view by Glasgow's infamous "bridge that goes nowhere " at Charing Cross.

A £73,000 modernisation "putting on the Ritz" makes this a lavishly comfortable, yet unpretentious pub. You'll have to go far to find a better display of both famous and obscure malts. Another unusual feature is that the 1/4 Gill is served at prices comparable with most other pubs who only offer 1/6th Gill - a proverbial whisky connoisseurs' paradise!

Surrounded by restaurants, pizza houses and bistros specialising in foreign food, the Ritz concentrates on very traditional dishes, although Chilli, lasagne and Burgers are also available. The daily special might be Sausage Hot Pot or Deep Fried Haddock, but the Scottish Steak Pie is said to be one of Glasgow's best. Meals are reasonably priced and portions are generous. As for the clientele, daytime business people are the most consistent regulars of a pub which attracts the passing trade, aged 18 to 80 plus.

ROCK GARDEN

73 Queen Street

TEL: 221 2200

Campbell's 70/-, Stella.

First opened in 1978 the Rock Garden was best known for its "French" Rock Restaurant. The restaurant today is in the basement and offers Potato Skins, Meatloaf & Hash Browns, Burgers and vegetarian food, all very reasonably priced. The fayre may not be in the same bracket as the former restaurant, but now it's within everyone's price range and it tastes good!

Frequented by students, musicians and a faithful following of young trendies, the Rock is a popular and often noisy pub, bursting with vitality always, and bursting at the seams on weekends.

Most pubs put on the occasional happy hour, not the Rock, they put their own "wheel of fortune" into action every half hour between 5 and 7 pm. Depending where the wheel stops, you might win two drinks for the price of one or pay "silly" prices for certain drinks and have a great laugh in the process.

A feature has to be the orange squeezing machine - watch your fresh oranges being squashed to a pulp! Choose from a range of 15 foreign beers and lagers.

Like most forward thinking hostelries, you can comfortably ask for tea or coffee at any time. Food is available between noon and 6pm and a new addition to the menu which must be tried are "subs", a long french bread roll, hot and filled with just about anything you would want.

For those of you seeking a colourful, lively pub of an evening or good food during the day, make your way to the Rock Garden and soak up the casual, but electric atmosphere.

ROTUNDA (NORTH)

28 Tunnel Street

TEL: 204 1238

Campbell's 70/-, Heineken, Stella.

Opened in December '87 the Rotunda is one of Glasgow's most unusual places to eat and drink. Converted from its previous function of transporting goods underneath the River Clyde, this structure is an astonishing three storey cylindrical building housing two bars and two restaurants.

The top floor consists of an extravagant up-market and terribly chic cocktail bar. The furnishings and decor are predominantly black and grey, with chrome and steel features. In contrast the music is soft and moody - Sade a speciality. The most outstanding feature of this stunning room is the domed ceiling with small inset lights representing stars in a midnight sky.

The south facing gallery windows

frame an excellent panoramic view over the Clyde, encompassing the Garden Festival site. Popular with diners awaiting their feast in the main restaurant, who are soothed into the mood by the proficient pianist. The main restaurant is equally chic with soft peach colours repeated through carpeting, wall coverings and fabrics. It has a partitioned area for functions and a live music set to suit the surroundings is a regular feature. A la carte French food is the speciality.

The Pizzeria on the first floor has a lively Italian atmosphere. Piped music keeps the mood cheery and even on a Monday night this section is close to its 150 seat capacity.

The ground floor wine bar, decorated in heavy dark wood with lots of brass, suggests the interior of an old sailing ship from Nelson's day. I had expected that some of the original "ticket office" or "lift shaft" features of the original building might have been retained, and was disappointed that none were; however, the bar achieves a strong connection with things naval, and this is quite appropriate. The main reception is bright, light and airy. The white floor tiling enhances the peach and off white walls and the tropical plants give the impression of a colonial style mansion house.

Although not the most inexpensive place in town it is well worth a visit.

SCARAMOUCHE

138 Elderslie Street

TEL: 333 9735

McEwan's, Beck's.

A strange concoction of very traditional decor, leggy barmaids and that rare atmosphere which accommodates conversation, even on weekends! So if you like the idea of a very quiet drink of a Saturday night and you like to be guaranteed a seat, make your way along to the top end of Elderslie Street.

The weekday custom is largely made up of those not so rare beasts, office workers from the Park Circus area. It can be very much a male domain. While male domination prevails, don't prejudge the staff, their service to other women customers was excellent - a feature not found in too many public houses!

Scaramouche provides a fairly comprehensive menu, combining traditional dishes with the option of the popular Chilli and Lasagne. Daily specials epitomise good quality and quantity and are available from 11am to 10 pm.

The large central bar houses the usual range of drinks with special promotions regularly featured. The main age range is 21 - 35 but it is the kind of pub where the attentive, efficient and welcoming staff make all customers relaxed. Live jazz is a monthly mid-week alternative to the background taped music which is normally in evidence.

Named after the French aristocrat, turned clown, who was guillotined, the Scaramouche is a fair reflection of the character.

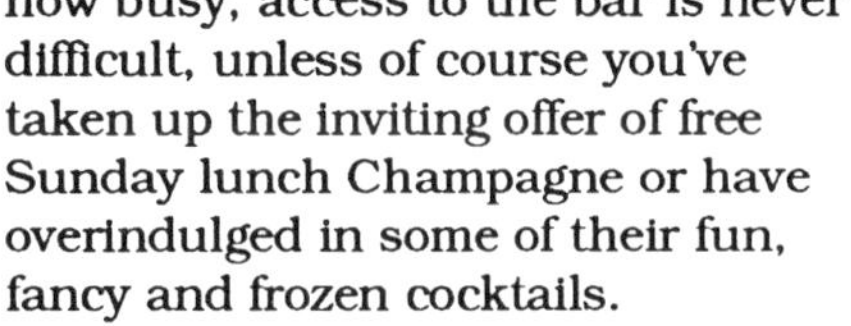

SHENANIGANS

351 Sauchiehall Street

TEL: 332 8205

Tartan Special, McEwan's 80/-, Beck's.

Opened in November, '87, Shenanigans introduced an exciting new concept to Glasgow....a place where anyone, of any age can eat or drink in surroundings which encourage both fun and relaxation. Fourth birthdays, retirement celebrations and office outings occur simultaneously in the cleverly designed peripheral restaurant areas, with staff taking their cue from customers as to how much or how little attention they desire. The staff epitomise the Oxford dictionary interpretation of "Shenanigans" frolicking, playing tricks, and are guaranteed to contribute to your particular celebration in such a way that you'll never forget it.

A raised central platform houses the enormous square bar, so no matter how busy, access to the bar is never difficult, unless of course you've taken up the inviting offer of free Sunday lunch Champagne or have overindulged in some of their fun, fancy and frozen cocktails.

If you take up their special lunchtime challenge, and have to wait more than 15 minutes for lunch - you won't have to pay for it! Attention to detail - the customer knows best - efficient, good humoured service - all are in evidence at Shenanigans.

The decor is warm and comfortable, using lots of natural wood and muted lighting. Specialising in Cajun cooking - try the Mardi Gras Chicken - the menu is diverse with unusual snacks, eg. Fried Cheese Sticks, Broccoli Bites and Sauted Shrimps.

THE GLASGOW

SLOAN'S

62 Argyle Arcade
108 Argyle Street

TEL: 221 8917

Alloa 70/-, Burton, Maclay's, Skol, Lowenbrau, XXXX.

Sloan's with its olde worlde charm, warm mahogany and etched glass, is said to be the oldest restaurant in Glasgow. It's origin dates back to 1797 when Glasgow's population was only eight thousand people. As a coffee house in those days it was the meeting point for the city's Tobacco Lords and Merchants, many of whom had their fashionable residences in Buchanan Street, and who enjoyed their sports of shooting partridges in Gordon Street and fishing for salmon and trout in the River Clyde.

At the turn of the century, the old ground floor restaurant became a lounge bar, which is now once again due for refurbishment. At the time of going to press work was about to start and is due to be completed by 1990.

Frequented by busy shoppers laden down with the day's purchases at lunchtimes and young shop workers and insurance salesmen and women in the evenings. Sloan's does not a bad pub lunch, for example, home made Steak Pie is amongst their range of traditional dishes. You could do much worse for this part of town.

SMITHS WINE BAR

47 West Nile Street

TEL: 221 4677

Tartan Special, McEwan's, Beck's, No 3.

This wine bar is well estab lished as a plush, tastefully decorated bar, frequented by the business community. The decor is subtle and the atmosphere one of confident relaxed conversation.

Like most establishments owned by Scottish & Newcastle, it has retained its individual character, benefitting from the absence of uniform features. Offering in excess of 25 wines, (as you would expect in a wine bar), including very palatable house wines, does not mean that your choice of beers, lagers, spirits and even Guinness is in any way restricted. Smiths carry seven foreign beers, No. 3 Real Ale and you can enjoy hot chocolate, coffee or tea at any hour. At the time of going to press, food is available between noon and 5pm, however this is likely to be extended into the evening.

The menu is particularly suited to vegetarian tastes, offering Quiche, Curried Pastas, Salads, Pate and Omelettes, but there are also meat dishes, so don't be disheartened. Meals are lower than average price range, and the freshness and visual appeal will generate an appetite.

39 STEPS

95 Union Street

TEL: 221 5020

Tennent's Beers.

Based on the site of Grant's once famous bookstore, the 39 Steps is a thriving city centre pub/restaurant. Situated alongside Central Station it caters for many different tastes. The massive interior is well laid out and tastefully furnished. Beer and whisky drinkers have nothing to fear here but the prices which are slightly above average. The bar boasts an immense selection of malt whiskies - the owner, John Waterson is quite an expert, although he doesn't actually drink the stuff himself. He can tell at a sniff one whisky from another and in fact, lectures on the subject around the world. Real ale is available, as well as non-alcoholic beers, a selection of wines or tea and coffee.

Snacks and full meals can be had throughout opening hours, ranging from Burgers through to Steak and the prices are fair. Meals are served in the restaurant, featuring a mock portion of the Forth Road Bridge, very appropriate, eh!

The only drawback is that the pub is very popular on weekends when it is filled to bursting point and the music is loud for the pre-disco set. A time to be avoided!

TIMES SQUARE

46 - 48 St Enoch Square

TEL: 221 6579

Alloa 70/-, XXXX, Skol, Lowenbrau.

Given the name American memorabillia is what you would expect to find in this pub, and you do. The walls are adorned with flags of American Baseball teams, photographs of famous players and other such decorations. As you enter you are faced with five large clocks which tell you the time in New York ,Toyko, Paris etc., or they did at some point in time, they no longer work. At the rear of the bar is Ed's Diner, which offers a good range of Mexican/American food.

In keeping with the theme, the back of the menu is a copy of the New York Times for 2nd October, 1952, although I'm not quite sure what the significance of the date is unless that's when the clocks stopped. The menu is a little pricey, but the portions are excessive, and several tasty vegetarian dishes are on offer. The restaurant motto is "If it ain't Ed's it ain't edible!".

The bar staff are neatly turned out in black waistcoats, white shirts and aprons, and provide quick and efficient service, and the beer ain't bad either.

The New York Times.

Copyright, 1952, by The New York Times Company.

NEW YORK, THURSDAY, OCTOBER 2, 1952.

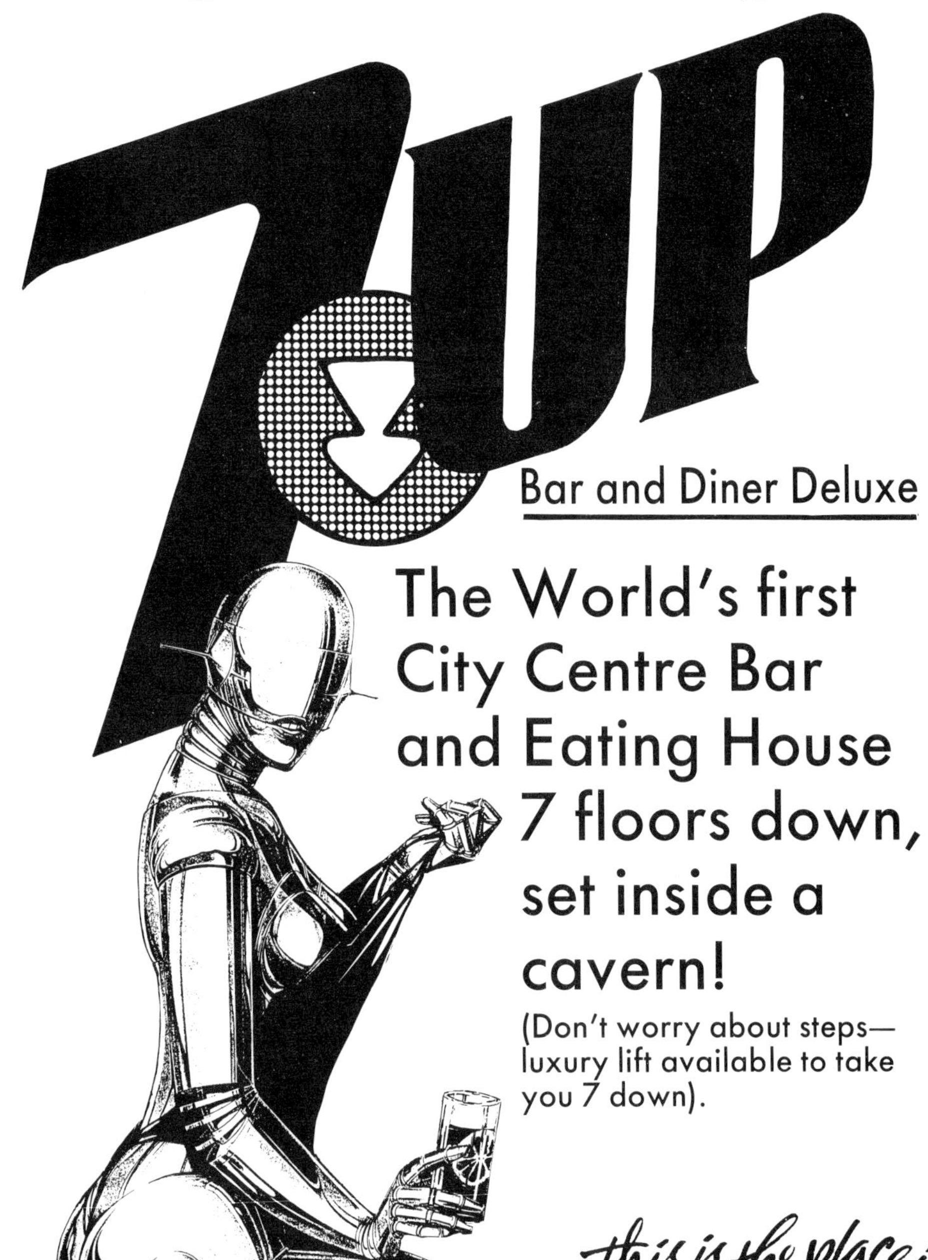
To open February '89
7UP
Bar and Diner Deluxe
The World's first
City Centre Bar
and Eating House
7 floors down,
set inside a
cavern!
(Don't worry about steps—
luxury lift available to take
you 7 down).
this is the place!
51 West Regent Street
Tel: 041-331 1980

1. ARAGON
2. ARLINGTON BAR
3. BONHAMS
4. CHIMMY CHUNGAS
5. CUL DE SAC
6. CURLERS BAR
7. DIVA BAR/RESTAURANT
8. DOUBLET
9. EXCHEQUER BAR
10. FINLAY'S
11. HALT BAR
12. LA TAVERNA
13. LAUTREC'S BRASSERIE
14. OBLOMOV
15. O'HENRYS CAFE/BAR
16. REID'S OF PERTYCK
17. STIRLING CASTLE
18. STUDIO ONE
19. TENNENT'S

RESTAURANTS

20. ASHOKA WEST END
21. BACK ALLEY
22. BASIL'S VEGETARIAN CAFE
23. CREPERIE
24. DI MAGGIO'S
25. SPAGHETTI FACTORY
26. UBIQUITOUS CHIP

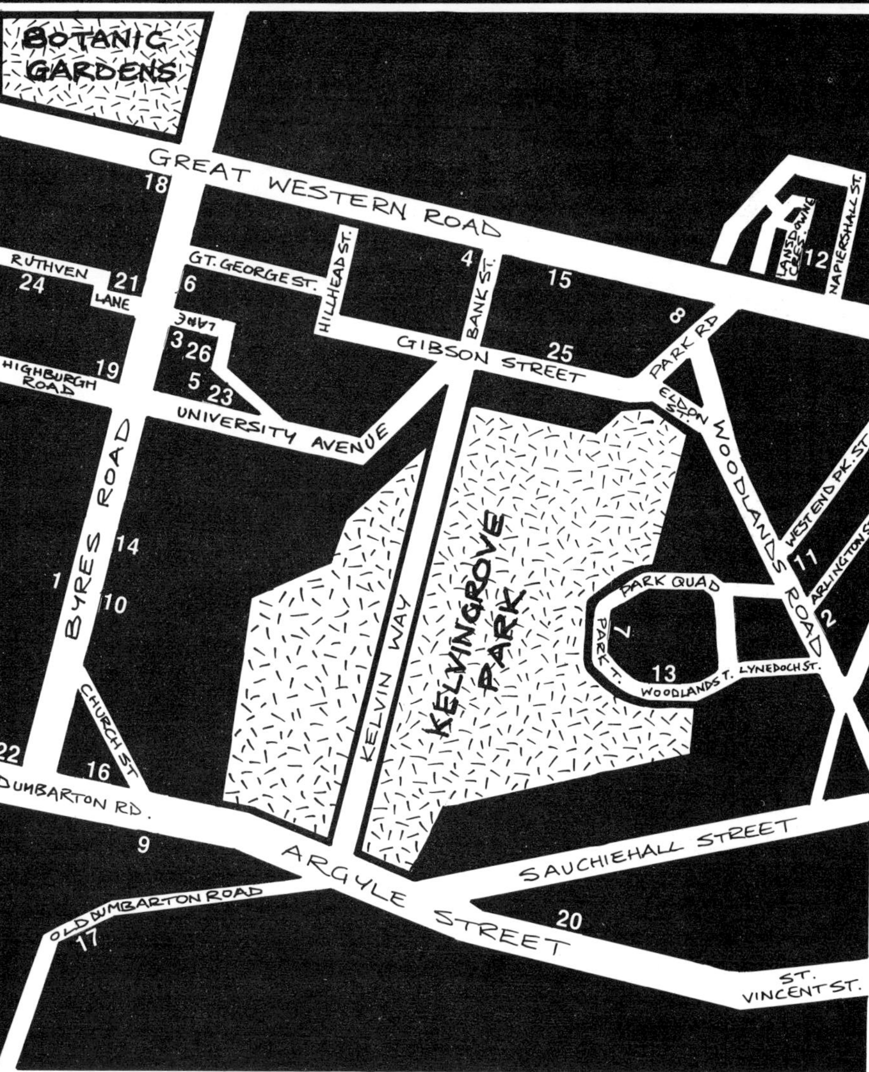

ARAGON

Byres Road

Byres Road has always been renowned for its impressive and varied selection of hostelries. However this attraction is difficult to grasp when you visit the Aragon. Not that it lacks originality, dullness is a very original feature in Byres Road - it just seems to lack everything else.

Like any local, the Aragon does have regulars, and regulars always have good reasons for coming back - in this case I can only imagine that they all have shares in the pub. That said, the very existence of the Aragon does make neighbouring bars look even better, so it does contribute something to the area .

In its favour, prices are well below the normal level of the west-end average, so in the same way that a take-home fish supper can be the best food in the world, a pint in the Aragon can be exactly what you want. The quality of the beer is without question. This pub has been in business for a long time and will probably continue for many years to come, so it must be doing something right. I just fail to see what that might be!

I would compare an evening in the Aragon with a journey on a number 59 bus (which has broken down and no-one told the passengers).

ARLINGTON BAR

Arlington Street

Situated at the corner of Arlington Street and Woodlands Road, this bar must qualify as one of the better oases for dedicated beer and spirits drinkers. At a time when many traditional Glasgow bars are losing their identity in a search for glamour and high profit margins, the Arlington is unchanged and hopefully will remain that way for a long time.

The foremost virtues of the bar are extraordinarily quick service regardless of how busy it is, excellent quality beer, cellar control coupled with a good range of beers, an interesting population mix between refugees from the Charing Cross office area and local residents (colourful in every sense of the word), and very fair prices.

Whilst it would be an exaggeration to describe the available food as a drawback, it is, as the Americans put it "strictly from hunger". The decor is classical Glasgow, with no frills at all. Music is restricted to those customers who find the spoken word inadequate to express their emotions.

A totally unpretentious, well managed and reasonably priced pub. Strongly recommended.

GLASGOW HAD OVER 130 CINEMAS OPEN DURING THE 1930'S. NOW IT HAS ONLY 5.

BONHAMS

194 Byres Road

TEL: 357 3424

Belhaven 80/-, Tartan Special, Beck's, XXXX, Tennent's, Stella.

If you've never spent the night in the foyer of an old picture house (cinema), now is your chance.

Bonhams is the refurbished foyer of the old Grosvenor picture house, which still operates from the rear of the block.

It is a small bar, but has a very pleasant atmosphere, generated by a unique combination of factors - friendly staff, an interesting and unusual gallery floor, a mix of clientele, and some excellent malt whisky.

Real ale and lager at average prices, spirits are good value and there are particularly attractive offers available on bottles of quite cheeky house wine.
Enjoy regular, very talented live music sets, and despite the pub being small, the decibel level is never overpowering.

The 6 - 8 pm cocktail "happy hour" is popular on weekdays and you can relax on a Sunday lunchtime with a newspaper and a hot chocolate.

A feature of the bar is the decor, modern stained glass, wall hung top hats, and even an old bicycle.

CHIMMY CHUNGAS

499 Great Western Road

TEL: 334 0884

Campbell's 70/-, Moosehead, Stella.

The facade of the old Coopers Finefare Building (complete with clock tower) is the first unusual feature of this Mexican cafe, bar & cantina. The interior is equally interesting, the whole area being split into three stepped levels.

The ground floor lounge is connected to the mezzanine restuarant by a wide spiral staircase. The middle floor is occupied by the main bar.

"Chimmy Chungas" is dervived from "Chimichangas" which are deep fried shredded beef or chicken Burritos, covered with red sauce, Guacamole and sour cream. If that sounds nice, there lots more! "Tampico" is lightly spiced chicken wrapped in two corn tortillas smothered in casa sauce and topped with sour cream and Guacamole. Other spicy dishes are Fajitas, Nachos & Tacos.

Mexican coffee is laced with Tequila, Kahlua & topped not with a Grolsh, but whipped cream. Bottled and canned beers served include Chimmy Chungas lager, Dos Equis, Superiore, Pacifico and Lone Star.

Decor is a reasonable if not startling attempt at genuine Mexican. Heavy patterned table cloths, wallmounted artifacts and a very rough "door mat" material carpet help create the image.

Service from the young informal staff is friendly enough, if not exactly "slick". Clientele is predominantly the 25 - 35 age group and jeans and rugby shirts are common garb. The house music is mostly rhythm & blues with occasional oldies - from Dylan to Robert Kray if you like.

The bar area serves reasonably priced lunches (including Alabama mud pie).

Overall the atmosphere is lively and Chimmy Chungas is definetely a hot spot in the West!

CUL DE SAC

46 Ashton Lane

TEL: 334 8899

McEwan's 80/-, Beck's, Harp.

This bar arose as a spin-off from the Creperie on the ground floor, and has inherited various features from its progenitor. These include a reasonably successful attempt to capture the French cafe-bar atmosphere and good quality food. Bar menus usually include some novel mixtures, and those tried were very successful.

The Cul De Sac is a young persons' bar and very popular. It is generally crowded after 9 pm and this results in extended periods spent waiting at the bar to be served. A natural aptitude in body swerving is a prerequisite if drinks are to be carried any distance!

A good range of beers, wines and spirits is available. Prices for both food and drink are what one would expect from this stylish establishment, i.e., substantially more than could be found in a more mundane environment.

A pleasant spot for an early evening meal and a quick gargle, particularly so if going on to the Grosvenor Cinema next door. Visits later on should be restricted to leisurely drinkers who like company.

RUMOUR HAS IT THAT A ROYAL CHARTER FROM KING CHARLES II ENABLED CURLERS TO SERVE DRINK AT ANY TIME.

CURLERS BAR

256 Byres Road

TEL: 334 1284

Tennent's Beers.

A pub which I have always thought can't make up its mind whether to be a trendy west-end bar or a "rough and tumble" pub. The result is that it achieves neither. Upstairs there are two bars which tend to be very busy, full of students and the usual colourful variety of west-end locals. Even the decor of each of these bars is a contradiction, with one being fairly plush whilst the other is decorated in tiled, hard cold materials. The latter is generally lively and this must have something more to do with the live jazz. I once had a pub lunch of "plastic" roast beef and had to chase the staff to pay for the privilege!

The downstairs lounge is equally as likely to become very boisterous at the weekend, so if you fancy the idea of a loud, carefree night out, this could be the place for you.

DIVA BAR/ RESTAURANT

7 Park Terrace

TEL: 332 3520

Campbell's 70/-, Stella, Heineken.

If you're beautiful or want to look at the beautiful, Diva is the shop window of Glasgow's "nouveau riche".

Incorporating a French a la carte restaurant & bar, everyone who is anyone comes to be seen in this "yuppie" haven. The Filo-fax/ American Express/ Porsche abound and if you're young and trendy Diva is for you.

The restaurant has 10 tables, with a capacity to seat 50 and offers a wide range of French cuisine & a special cafe night menu. Prices are reasonably competitive and the cocktail list is quite extensive.

The decor is modern - chromed steel, tiled floor, neon wall lights & framed graphic prints.
Taped background music is mainly soul & charts and the clientele is strictly fashion conscious. A strong regular clientele, so visitors are generally more comfortable in a group. The staff are young, informal & friendly and a stool bar invites casual chatting when the establishment is not busy. Thursday, Friday & Saturday evenings are extremely popular. I once knew a model who didn't go to Diva's!

DOUBLET

74 Park Road

TEL: 334 1982

Beck's, Heineken, Harp.

Having just celebrated it's silver anniversary, the Doublet bar looks forward to the next quarter century through its new curtains. Renowned throughout Glasgow as a place containing more disputatious punters than Venice, it also contains arty humour and a warm welcome for strangers. Where else can you find Taggart arguing with a real police inspector about flying ducks?....or drink the best pint of Murphy's in town?

For those who don't know, a doublet is a close fitting garment for the upper part of the body and while unlike Hamlet with his "doublet all unbraid", the ladies of the long bar will serve you "measure for measure" or "as you like it".

The Doublet provides a range of real ales as well as a small but selective choice of malt whiskies. Meals include snacks as well as Lasagne and Chilli.

Overall the Doublet can be described as a small parochial type of hostelry willing to open its doors to the thirsty stranger.

EXCHEQUER BAR

59 Dumbarton Road

TEL: 334 3301

Dryborough's 70/-, XXXX, Skol.

On entering this west-end bar there is a tangible olde worlde atmosphere due in no small part to the lighting, or the lack of it, to be more precise. Opened seven years ago and situated near the foot of Byres Road, on Dumbarton Road, the Exchequer is a pub to sit and relax in.

Privately owned by Jack Grant Kinnell, it boasts a good variety of beers including foreign lagers, wines and some malt whiskies as well as the usual spirits, tea and coffee. Meals are to be had between 12 noon and 9 pm. Choose from a menu which is light on the pocket, although fairly substantial. Unusually, children are welcomed, if you are eating.

This facility is spacious, with an attractive upstairs gallery area and a beer garden, the latter being a rare commodity in Glasgow. The pub's claim to fame is its "art nouveau" facade which is listed as of special architectural interest. Also open on Sundays the Exchequer caters for all ages and styles without any particular category of customer prevailing.

FINLAY'S

94 Byres Road

TEL: 339 7409

Tennent's Beers.

This is a rather surprising oasis of calm in the bustle of Byres Road. A rather uninspiring brick exterior is balanced by a very pleasant interior. The muted browns & beiges of the furnishings, floor tiles & natural looking wood panelling are complemented by clusters of upwardly glowing lamps. The light bulbs and shades produce a very relaxing warm amber glow.

There is an abundance of pine shaded wood panelling on both bar and walls. This would normally be rather overwhelming but is successfully balanced by a series of regularly positioned bronze smoked glass mirrors. The glass element is furthered by the many rectangular windows forming the two outside walls of the bar.

The wall ranges have a simple design of clean angular lines. An unobtrusive combination of textures, shapes & colour combined with curved fixed seating prompts chat between customers.

The house music is melodic pop played at just the right volume.

For those who like propping up the bar a lone brass footrest is a nice touch, and the design of the rest of the bar is also very attractive. A feature overhead glasses rack runs the bar length, and behind the gantry are rather interesting etched glass mirrors.

At the far end of the room there are steps up to the small cosy semi-circular lounge area.

Smartly dressed staff will serve you your pleasure in drinks. Prices are reasonable and clientele are of a very mixed age group. Dress is casual but a door sign advertised "no bikers jackets or work boots"!

HALT BAR

106 Woodlands Road

TEL: 332 1210

Heineken, Stella, Moosehead.

hugely popular pub located on the outskirts of Glasgow's west-end. It is an established traditional pub run by Whitbreads. Despite several recent renovations the brewers have stuck to the traditional decor and resisted the common trend of Yuppification with over priced beers and fake mahogany panelling bedecked with the ubiquitous black & white photographs of Glasgow scenes.

The bar is preserved in its original horseshoe shape with a minimum of decoration or memorabilia; even the television is discreetly placed above and just inside the main entrance preventing any noisy intrusion to the intense intellectual debates going on underneath. The lounge impresses as spacious but intimate with various open-ended snug compartments. It also has a large open section catering for the regular jazz and rhythm & blues bands which entertain on a Tuesday & Thursday night.

The pub offers a full range of pub meals as well as snacks catering for the hungry but not the discerning eater. The gantry boasts at least 30 malt whiskies as well as a range of real ales supplemented by imported high alchohol lagers, draught & bottled.

Overall the Halt's attractiveness lies in the unpretentious hordes that frequent it whether to sample the live entertainment or merely to enjoy an evening amongst friends.

PUB GUIDE

LA TAVERNA

7a Lansdowne Crescent

TEL: 339 7128

Campbell's 70/-, Stella, Heineken, Castle Eden.

Formerly the well-loved "Raga muffin" Bar, La Taverna while new in name still retains most of the character which made it so popular. Off the beaten track it is not the kind of place that you would come across by accident. It is to be found in a basement and is "well lived in". Decor, fixtures and fittings are an unusual clutter of styles. A stag's head mounted over an imitation log fire, cartoons share wall space with imitation dutch masters, but the strangest of all has to be the imitation tree coated with plastic ivy! A bar dominated by locals, the atmosphere is one of comfortable familiarity.

A small lounge area off the main bar accommodates lively discussion on every conceivable subject - it is nice to hear that the art of conversation is not dead! Housed at the rear of the establishment is a particularly good Italian restaurant, where fish is a speciality in addition to many pasta dishes. Seating around 80, their capacity is high as will be your appetite for large portions and reasonable prices.

So, if you want to meet some "real" west-enders in an atmosphere which is so relaxed it is almost horizontal, enjoy a filling plate of pasta and listen to the late, great Jim Reeves on the P.A., try La Taverna.

LAUTREC'S BRASSERIE

14 Woodlands Terrace

TEL: 332 7013

Whitbread Export, Heineken, Stella.

Once the trendiest bar in Glasgow, Lautrec's has settled down to a normal life! Whilst it still retains a rather fashionable atmosphere, the clientele now encompasses a broader age group, from 30-50 years. Framed mono-colour graphic photo prints adorn the walls and small round tables and wicker weave chairs are scattered around comfortable leather settees.

The bar menu is extensive and includes Mandarin or Melon Cocktail, Chicken Liver Pate and Stuffed Mushrooms. Main courses offer Burgers, Chicken, Lamb, Lasagne and Steak, whilst the sweet menu has Pecan Crumble and Fudge Sauce Ice Cream. The Pecan Crumble is a favourite. Stilton and Brie are served with Oatcakes, Apple and Celery. The food is reasonably priced and of good quality, therefore very popular with the business community at lunchtime.

One of this establishment's main claims to fame is their range of over 100 wines - not only the usual and popular, but the very special too. Try a '78 chateau Figeac, St Emilion, Ler Grand Cru Classe, or why not finish off your lunch with a classic '66 Croft Port, served by the 2 ounce glass or decanter.

The Brasserie section is to be found through the back of the lounge and up the stairs, offering a fairly limited a la carte menu at reasonable prices. If thinking of going at lunchtime you should book a table in advance as it is quite small.

Staff in Lautrec's are surprisingly young and inexperienced, considering the clientele. It would be wise to impersonate a "regular" if you need attentive service! Try to look as though you have just parked your Range Rover outside and are just dying for a bottle of Perrier Jouet '81 Belle Epoque!

N BIJDRAGE?
NOOIT!!
agenda
PAPUCSKA
t/m ZA 14/04/84 20.15u
EINE KOMEDIE
HULP
IS!

THE GLASGOW

OBLOMOV

116/122 Byres Road

TEL: 334 2666

Campbell's 70/-, Heineken, Moosehead, Stella.

With wood panelled floor and bar this bar/cafe/restaurant has a definite cosmopolitan ambience. Attracting a large number of tourists, both British and foreign, there is a relaxed holiday atmosphere, aided by the availability of Scrabble, Backgammon and good quality newspapers.

The ceiling is covered in Dutch posters of old and new movies. Yellow stippled walls and rich carpeted upholstery on the couches and glass topped tables create the impression that Oblomov has been around far longer than the 17 months since it opened. Divided into two separate parts, there is quite a difference between the bar and restaurant. Very crowded at weekends, the bar plays host to a young, student oriented crowd, catering to their needs by playing the latest club and chart sounds. A good bar to make new friends in. In contrast, the bar/restaurant next door has a more mature clientele.

Management are currently considering holding a Dutch evening fortnightly, playing the latest Dutch chart sounds.

The restaurant menu, as you might expect, is Dutch oriented, and changes regularly. Breakfast is served from 10 am - 12 noon, and you can choose as little as a Croissant with butter and marmalade or a full continental breakfast. At lunchtime or in the evening try "Polpette" Italian Meat Loaf, served with salad and bread or Steak in a Mushroom and Cream Sauce. Definitely "goed eten".

At the time of going to press the owners were about to launch a new restaurant, opposite the Art Galleries, which should prove to be as successful as Oblomov.

The Name Oblomov, is no doubt from the '79 movie of the same name, or perhaps from the novel about a lazy, daydreaming landowner who is forced to face his life squarely when he falls in love.

THE LAST PERSON TO BE HANGED IN PUBLIC IN GLASGOW WAS DR. EDWARD PITCHARD IN 1865, BEFORE A CROWD OF 80,000.

O'HENRYS CAFE/BAR

445 Great Western Road

TEL : 339 1275

Campbell's 70/-, Heineken, Moosehead, Stella, Castle Eden.

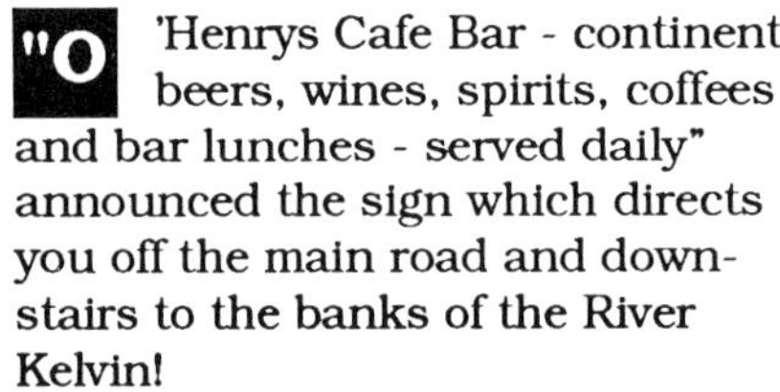

"O'Henrys Cafe Bar - continental beers, wines, spirits, coffees and bar lunches - served daily" announced the sign which directs you off the main road and downstairs to the banks of the River Kelvin!

On warm summer evenings you can sit outside on the riverbank, beneath the trees, enjoying the sound of the river swirling below. A converted bridge arch, this extremely unusual bar looks as if it has been hewn out of the living rock. The front section is a highly arched "cavern" with around thirty basic wooden tables set on a planked wooden floor. There is no decor and no fixtures at all, bar a couple of small wall lights. It does however have character.

Through from the "arch" is the actual bar with small lounge. Again simple and straightforward is the style. A feature is a large oak barrel, normally filled with peanuts - you help yourself and nobody seems to mind what you do with the shells.

Bar lunches are also on offer and dishes such as Quiche, Pies and Baked Potatoes are typial.
Jazz is featured regularly with live acts in the front section, piped over the house P.A. system.

The clientele is 20 - 35 in age and it is popular with third and fourth year students from the nearby Glasgow University. The mood is quite relaxed, bar staff are young and quite efficient, and groups of people engaged in light conversation is usual - outwith the live jazz, of course! Wear your oldest jeans!

REID'S OF PERTYCK

80 Dumbarton Road

TEL: 334 8012

Tennent's Beers, Maclay's, Stella, Moosehead.

Reid's has most of the qualities you would expect from a traditional west-end bar, most importantly, a comfortable atmosphere. The cost of food and drinks is more than reasonable and regulars, (some of whom have been frequenting this pub for the best part of its 50 year life) will be happy to support these claims. Strong links with Partick Thistle F.C. and the industrious Clydeside in its heyday will be the storylines of any one of the many older regulars.

GLASWEGIANS THOUGHT THE FIRST POLICE FORCE STARTED IN 1778 WASN'T WORTH THE EXPENSE. IT LASTED 3 YEARS.

Taped but unobtrusive music, mostly charts and rock n' roll, plays in the background, attracting those in their 20's and 30's to the lounge , whilst the bar's clientele encompasses all age groups. Nice to see such blatant glorification of the working classes, displayed through framed photographs of industrial scenes.

Named after Miller Reid, the owner, Reid's benefits from being exactly what it has been for the last 50 years - a quality, straightforward pub.

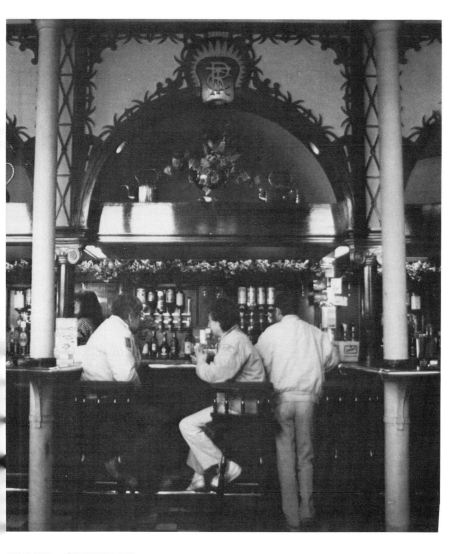

STIRLING CASTLE

90 Dumbarton Road

TEL: 339 8132

Tennent's Beers, Belhaven 80/-.

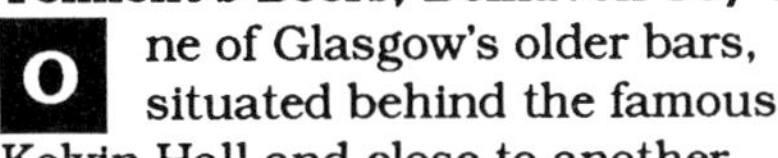

One of Glasgow's older bars, situated behind the famous Kelvin Hall and close to another landmark, the Art Galleries and Museum.

The "Castle" went through a major facelift and refurbishment early in '88 and has really changed in every respect, except the name! Decor is a jumble of styles, colours, patterns and ornaments. A full-dress kilt uniform of an Argyle and Sutherland Highlander is displayed in a glass case on one wall, a reproduction "Ming" vase sits next to an earthenware cider jug, a pot of plastic foliage, an imitation musket, a four foot high statue, ceramic sherry barrow - the Stirling Castle has it all!

The clientele is predominantly local and regular. Everyone seems to know everyone else and the age span is wide, mother and son, father and daughter, uncles and inlaws, drink, laugh and argue together. The variety of fashions sported is also rather bizarre, aunties in frocks rub bare shoulders with brickies in baseball boots. Piped popular music is played at three-quarters' volume and everyone talks much louder than is actually neccessary. The whole mad place is really very enjoyable, full of laughing and animated characters, with friendly and efficient barmen.

There is also a small restaurant to seat around 30 off the bar and meals are served all day.

STUDIO ONE

Byres Road

Very much a student domain, Studio One is the first "watering hole" if venturing on a pub crawl down Byres Road. Located at a side entrance of the Grosvenor Hotel, it offers spacious surroundings with pleasant decor. Beers are well priced and draught Beck's increases its' appeal. Not a pretentious place by anyone's standards - a combination of good food, good beer and atmosphere it is the kind of place where a few drinks would go down well, although with so many alternatives in the vicinity, I can't imagine staying there all evening.

Food is unstartling but acceptable, all in all, a place where young people meet other young people.

TENNENT'S BAR WAS GRANTED A LICENCE IN 1887, ALTHOUGH GLASGOW UNIVERSITY OPPOSED THE APPLICATION.

TENNENT'S

Byres Road/Highburgh Road

Tennent's Beers, Greenmantle, Theakston's Old Peculiar.

Situated at the crossroads of Byres Road and Highburgh Road, Tennent's Bar cannot be overlooked. If you are intending some serious drinking, this is probably as good a place as any to be, for Tennent's is very much an old style stand at-the-bar-and-drink-pub.

Quite often it can be five deep around the long, horseshoe shaped bar. Stand for a minute and watch, you will witness an unusually successful scene of beer consumption. There is plenty to choose from - Tennent's 70 & 80/-, Theakston's Old Peculiar Real Ale, Greenmantle, Lager, Export and Guinness. The prices are quite inexpensive, as expense is spared in so many other departments. Decor and furnishings are basic, though the many groups of young and old debate loudly in all corners, seemingly blind to the more material aspects.

The clientele is very much the Glasgow "punter" and the bar attracts those who are "in for the night", particularly students, courtesy of the prices! Basic bar snacks are served but don't expect the Ritz! Some bring their dogs along and unless these canines decide to liven things up a bit, no-one pays them any heed.

Most regulars are probably unaware of it, but the ceiling sports a most unusual cornice, highly ornate moulding in a bizarre layout of squares. This is all supported by unevenly spaced pillars, topped with gold painted leaves. Cheap and rather nasty two tiered chandeliers illuminate the whole bar - which itself is an odd shape - students of architecture have been known to go insane in this pub.

The bar staff are efficient in their role of providing beer to dry throats, but if you want a conversation, bring a friend!

1. BABBITY BOWSTER
2. BLACKFRIARS
3. CIRCLE BISTRO & THE GODS
4. DRAWING ROOM
5. FIXX
6. GRANNY BLACK'S
7. JOHNNY SCOBIE'S
8. JOHN STREET JAM
9. MITRE BAR
10. SARACEN HEAD
11. TOLBOOTH
12. TRON THEATRE
13. VICTORIA BAR
14. ZHIVAGO'S

RESTAURANTS

15. BLUE NOTE
16. CAFE GANDOLFI
17. CAFE (WAREHOUSE)
18. COLONIAL
19. FIRE STATION
20. MILLER STREET CATERING CO.

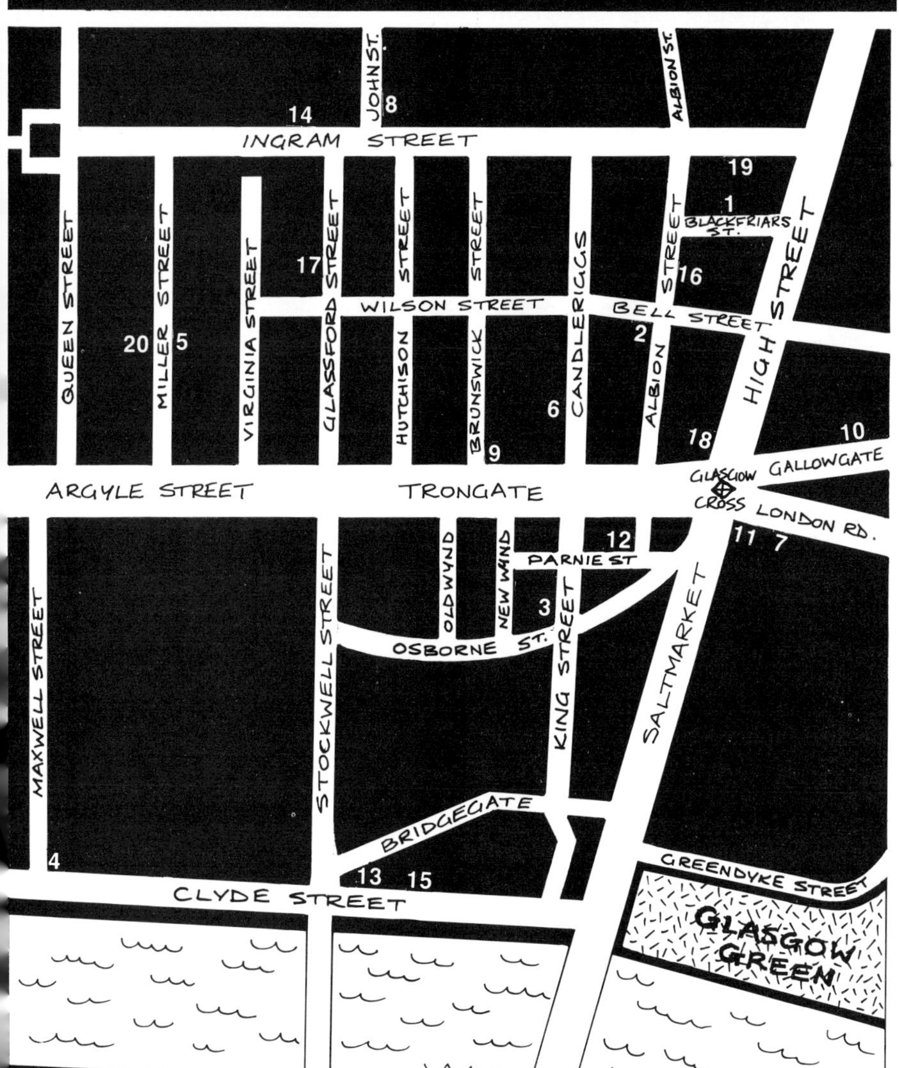

BABBITY BOWSTER

16/18 Blackfriars Street

TEL: 552 5055

Tennent's Beers, Porter, Maclay's.

1985 heralded the opening of this cafe/bar/restaurant/ hotel, set in the middle of the flourishing Merchant City, and no Glasgow guide would be complete without a review of it.

Explanation of the name itself is a common talking point in this comfortably stylish establishment, but with Fraser Laurie as proprietor, there is no need for conversation prompts. Monks are famed for their brewing and distilling skills and it is therefore quite appropriate that this beautifully refurbished Adams' 18th Century Town House is on the site of a former monastery! Babbity's has justifiably been praised in culinary and architectural journals alike.

The menu offers patrons a choice of well priced snacks and a full range of Scottish and Celtic dishes with an international influence. A favourite with the authors is the Vegetable Bake, priced at £3.45 and the imaginative fish and meat dishes which are unique to Babbity's.

Music, theatre and painting are strongly associated with Babbity's and regular events, including monthly poetry and musical sessions, offer an excellent night out.

You can enjoy a wide range of drinks, whether your preference is for real ale, capuccino or champagne at most hours of the day, and although over rowdy behaviour is rare (warm yet uninhibited being the norm) the proprietor has been known to "turn a blind eye"!

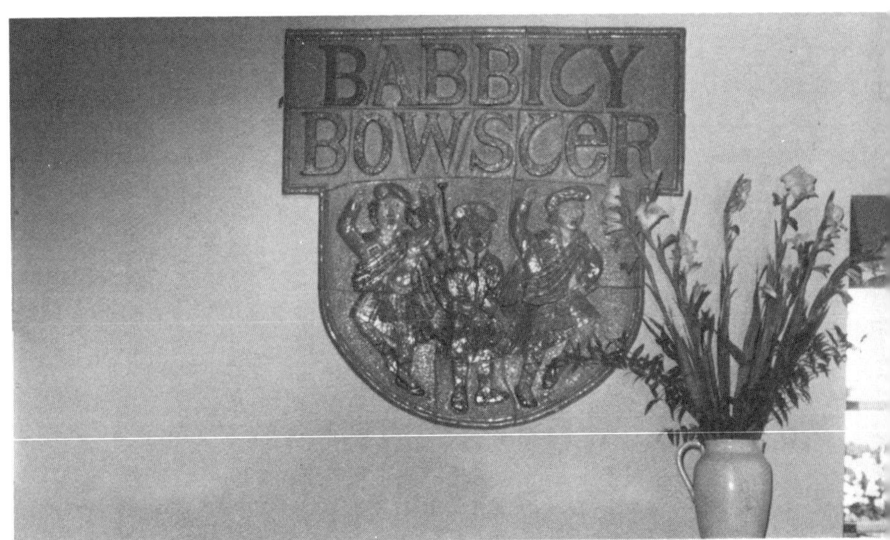

BLACKFRIARS

36 Bell Street

TEL: 552 5924

Dryborough's, XXXX, Burton, Maclay's, Belhaven.

None of your Yuppies or Dinkys in this reasonably clean well run pub. A healthy mix of customers, with live jazz and folk music on Thursday evenings through until Sundays. Good cheap bar lunches. Choose from home made soup, a range of Burgers and Baked Potatoes, Chilli and Quiche. I've often taken my mum & dad here for lunch!

Some beautiful large specially crafted brass Blackfriars mirrors provide character to this otherwise uninspiring pub. Popular for its range of real ales, wines and malt whiskies. The pub plays host to regular "Malt of the Month" promotion evenings. As one local said, the drink only hurts your head when you hit the pavement! A worthwhile pub in the older tradition.

CIRCLE BISTRO & THE GODS

50 - 60 King Street

TEL: 552 4289

Campbell's 70/-, Heineken, Stella, Furstenberg.

Opened in Autumn '87, yet another establishment contributing to the revitalisation of this part of the city, providing a service to the incoming dwellers with more money than sense. Following suit with other Bistros the bar is tastefully decorated with rich wood and stained glass. A raised gallery area with piano suggests that regular ivory tickling takes place here. So far the bar has failed to establish regular custom and probably does best from the Tron theatre goers, however the live folk music sets have proven to be popular, and sing-a-long sessions are on the increase!

The Gods restaurant menu offers traditional Scottish dishes such as Haggis and Neeps and Steak a la carte. It should offer something to suit your palate, including vegetarian dishes, all at reasonable prices. A pub with a modern image which complements the growing arts and crafts presence in the area.

THE DRAWING ROOM
'a new approach'
214 clyde st glasgow
248 4077

THE DRAWING ROOM

214 Clyde Street

TEL: 204 0352

Alloa 70/-, XXXX, Skol, Lowenbrau.

In what used to be the head quarters of the Iona Community, the Drawing Room fronts the Clyde Walkway. What was once a high - ceilinged series of offices has been beautifully converted, with an enormous square bar in the centre of the floor, raised seating areas at the panoramic windows and a gallery floor running around 3 walls. Warm wall coverings, dark bamboo furniture and some fascinating prints confirm the luxury of the Drawing Room.

The owner and staff are warm, outgoing and forward thinking. If the customer wants something they will do all they can to accommodate it. Reputed to be the largest gay bar in Scotland, it certainly smashes the sterotypes in a comfortable, constructive and light-hearted atmosphere!

Apart from "real ale", you can ask for any kind of beverage, whether hot chocolate, outrageous cocktails or anything in between and find that the price is cheaper than average for Glasgow's city centre.

Live Jazz, cabaret, 70's, and classical music all feature regularly and a D.J. is in residence on Thursdays evenings through to Sundays.

Active, noisy, busy, alive and energetic are the words to describe an evening in the Drawing Room. I suspect that once you've visited you'll find it hard to drag yourself away!

FIXX

86 Miller Street

TEL: 248 2859

Campbell's 70/-, Stella, Heineken, Moosehead.

Although probably best known for the quality of "live" bands that perform there, Fixx is a refurbished "jewellery store" which hit the headlines, courtesy of a famous robbery. The decor cannot be categorised as no single feature is in keeping with the next! The formula works - I still see "new" photographs, graffiti or antique commercial ads, and I've been eating and drinking there since it opened in '84.

Fixx has a reputation for promoting "up and coming" bands - Deacon Blues first gig in '86 took place there, when they shared the bill with Hue and Cry and Wet, Wet, Wet. So if you like good live music and like to be a few paces in front, visit Fixx! It may seem a strange mixture, but Fixx also focusses on Scottish and Irish popular music, Reggae and Jazz.

On the food front you can choose a light snack or a full meal, including Italian, Mexican, French and American dishes. The chilli is not for the faint hearted and would feed two people easily! If you're hungry visit Fixx between noon and 5pm. After 5pm it gets pretty busy, especially on Wednesdays, when you are guaranteed live music.

Although a fairly large bar, the Fixx is not too big to be impersonal, the split level floors, art nouveau figures, invading rhino, full wall collages and friendly bar staff ensure that it is very welcoming. Only the sexist photographs mar my enjoyment of this otherwise great bar.

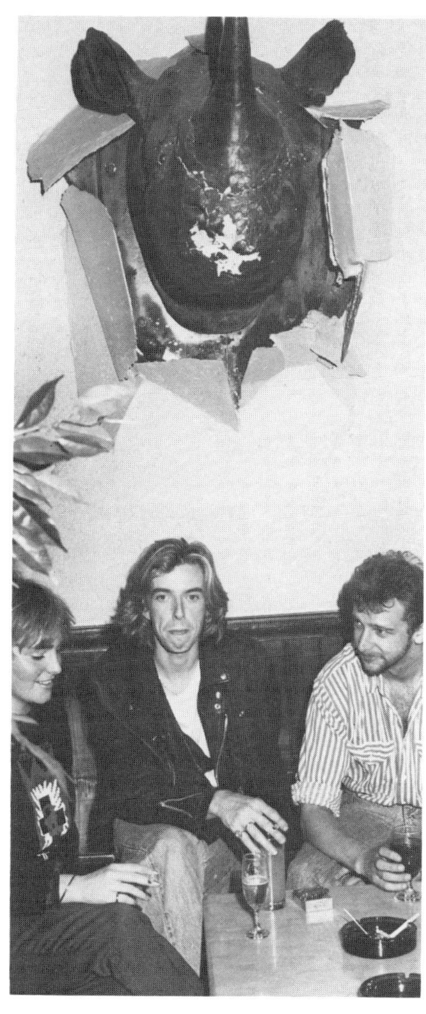

ROBERT BURNS STAYED AT THE BLACKBULL INN IN 1747 AND 1748, AT THE CORNER OF ARGYLE STREET AND VIRGINIA STREET.

GRANNY BLACK'S

55/57 Candleriggs

TEL: 552 2470

Alloa, Dryborough's, Skol, XXXX.

A famous traditional pub, first established in Candleriggs in 1820, moved to its present site in 1970. Granny Black's is small, unpretentious, and decidedly straightforward. So if you yearn for the days when a pub was just a pub, head down to Granny Black's for good honest beer and substantial affordable pub grub. Unlike modern pubs, food is only available between 11.30am - 2.30pm and 3.15 - 4.30pm and contrary to the trend in "the trade" you won't be able to have tea or coffee. Whilst some may frown on these retained characteristics of old, regulars welcome them, alongside traditional Glasgow patter, and, on occasion, some serious drinking sessions. Witness the recent headlines concerning private functions, when one "risque" event got a little out of hand!

The favourite food on offer is "mince & tatties" closely followed by "hot roast beef" which at just over £2 is the most expensive item on the menu.

You'll find the prices at Granny Black's are amongst the cheapest in the city, both for pub grub and drink! Given the growth in plush, designer diners/bistros, Granny Black's is a surviving example of an ordinary Glasgow pub. No frills, no airs, no graces, just a simple, straightforward hostelry.

JOHNNY SCOBIE'S

26 - 30 London Road

TEL: 552 6863

Tennent's Beers, Maclay's.

At first sight you might think that this is a small old fashioned sleazy Glesga pub, as it has a narrow and deceiving frontage underneath the arches. You'd be wrong! Once inside you discover that the 1850 Victorian built railway arches have been cleverly upgraded, managing to retain the original structure and capture the natural lighting to good effect.

The pub has strong links with the folk music circuit and is a regular venue for live entertainment, both planned and spontaneous. As you might expect where there is folk music, there is also real ale, not only that but the CAMRA executive committee hold their meetings there. Scobie's keep a minimum of three real ales and they give house room to a guest pump. There's also an impressive range of malt whisky, wines and scrumpy. Neil, the manager, will even prepare a hot toddy on request, in fact I imagine that there isn't a limit to his ingenuity in accommodating customers' requests.

If you're hungry the menu includes Mixed Grills, Scampi and Chicken dishes, but the speciality is Steak, which can be grilled or charcoaled. The Striploin Steaks are the most expensive dish on the menu at an exorbitant £3.25! Food is available between 12 noon and 8pm except Sunday evenings, but be warned, the portions are enormous. All in all, a pub to include on your list.

JOHN STREET JAM

18 John Street

TEL: 552 3801

Campbell's 70/-, Heineken, Stella, Moosehead.

Once the Hutcheson School, this listed building close to the City Chambers now houses the John Street Jam. Inside its owners have attempted to recreate the glamour and atmosphere of the deep south, that's California not London! They have spared nothing in refurbishing the interior with lavish paintings, which look like they might have come from the sets of "Gone with the Wind", carved balustrade, and a mezzanine floor which accommodates the restaurant. The menu features original Cajun food, which seems to be coming popular in Glasgow. Boasting real Alligator tail, (although no one that I know has actually been

served this delicacy), to gourmet Burgers, all at a price that you would expect for the Merchant City.

The ground floor hosts a large well staffed rectangular bar, with comfortable booths surrounding it. Live jazz, in keeping with the theme, is offered every Saturday and Sunday lunchtime.

On the edge of the Merchant City, the John Street Jam is fast overcoming its ambiguous frontage, which, protected by local planning controls, cannot be changed. This should be one pub that will outlive many of the others that have sprung up in this part of the city. Well worth a visit.

MITRE BAR

12 Brunswick Street

TEL: 552 3764

Tennent's Beers, Maclay's.

Arthur, who's 83, is reputed to have been Paul Newman's stand-in for the movie "The Hustler" sits in the corner of the Mitre bar which was here long before Arthur was born. Established over 100 years ago, the coffin-shaped gantry and Victorian bar are some of the many original features that still remain in this bar. The one thing that looks out of place is the telephone at the entrance, amidst a 1950's radio and a sign that reminds "gentlemen no swearing aloud".

A small very comfortable pub, frequented by many of the local worthies of the Saltmarket. There is also an excellent range of over 50 malt whiskies and over 40 different bottled beers in stock. For those of you who want to taste quality drinks and a little of Glasgow's traditional culture, a visit to the Mitre will ensure that both aims are satisfied.

  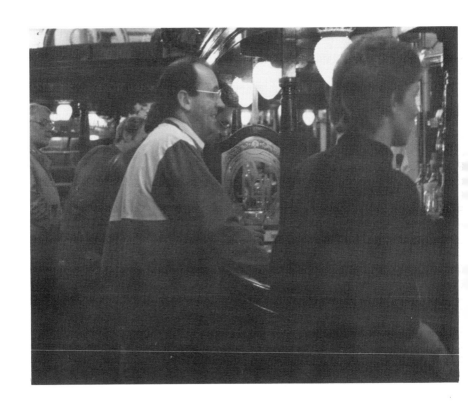  

SARACEN HEAD

Gallowgate

The "Sarry Heid" as it is affectionately known is one of the last ordinary working men's pubs to survive in the city. One of the oldest and best known pubs it started out life as an hotel named after an ancient Inn of London, by Robert Tennent, the original proprietor. The London Inn stood in Snow Hill in the 12th Century in honour of St. Thomas of Canterbury, whose maternal grandfather was a Saracen. The Inn once accommodated Johnson and Boswell after their famous highland jaunt. The Title Deeds go back as far as 1720, although the present building dates from 1755. At that time the Inn comprised a tavern, inn, assembly room, blacksmith's shop, coachhouse and could accommodate one hundred horses. The site is now occupied by truncated tenements from a quite different era.

Glaswegians probably recognise the Saracen Head more readily through Billy Connolly's reference to it being the location for the "Last Supper". Across the road from Glasgow's Barras market, the Sarry Heid has been in the same family since 1788. Angus Ross who owns the bar is himself of massive stature, equal to the pub's fame, although a quiet and courteous man. Four types of cider are available, two draught sherries and the ever popular Eldorado can be consumed on the premises or "kerried oot".

A bar full of short, animated men in flat hats and overcoats, always with a story to tell. You'll learn more about Glasgow's history in this pub than in any other. Let's hope that the revitalisation and gentrification of this part of our city does not threaten this breathing museum, and popular hostelry.

THE TOLBOOTH THAT WAS ORIGINALLY THE TOWN JAIL IS 126 FEET HIGH AND WAS BUILT IN 1738.

THE TOLBOOTH

11 Saltmarket

TEL: 552 4149

Tennent's Beers, Furstenberg.

Once a real spit and sawdust pub, the Tolbooth has become a casual, friendly establishment. Famed now for its generous and satisfying portions of Jumbo Sausage, Chips and Beans, currently receiving rave reviews in the Glasgow Herald, Egon Ronay, etc.. The other main attractions being real ale and live folk music . During the day you can expect to find all sorts of customers, but the evenings are dominated by "folky" types.

On a good Friday night a few musicians with tin whistles and guitars will begin to congregate in a corner of the bar, by the end of the evening they will have taken over with tambourines and banjos. Food is served until it runs out and staff will always try to accommodate your every wish. A good pub in the old tradition, but watch out for the television which can tend to dominate at tea time.

TRON THEATRE

64/69 Parnie Street

TEL: 552 3748

McEwan's 80/-, Beck's.

This bar was once the original Tron Theatre, with performances conducted on the raised platform at the rear. It now houses a larger than life statue of Robert Burns and several tables designed for those of us who like to see what's going on in the place. Since '78 the bar has been a club for members and patrons. Now open to all and sundry, a regular pursuit of locals is star spotting, attempting to recognise characters from "Take the High Road" and other well known Scottish productions. Frequented by the famous and "would be famous" the

bar offers a good variety of red and white wine and foreign bottled beers. A broad range of daily specials is popular at lunchtimes and in the evenings. Choose from a selection of Baked Potatoes, vegetarian dishes and some interesting Cheeses. An attraction is the live Jazz music on Sunday afternoons, but avoid the bar on Mondays as you will find it closed.

A beautiful mahogany bar stretches the entire length of the room, and aproned bar staff serve customers in a leisurely fashion. The Compass Gallery has free use of the walls to exhibit work. No condom machine however as it had to be removed because of regular break-ins. Could this be the work of poverty stricken, aids-conscious artistes and performers? A lively "arty" atmosphere most evenings, although quieter in between theatre performances.

THE VICTORIA BAR

157/9 Bridgegate

TEL: 552 6040

Tennent's Beers, Maclay's, Theakston's Best Bitter, Greenmantle.

Nothing much to look at from the outside, you might make the mistake of walking past the Vicky bar. Venture inside to discover the stuff of successful pubs. Owner/manager Gerry Davis easily and naturally ensures good service, an excellent pint, the best in folk music and good basic pub grub. Visit the Victoria Bar on a second occasion and you'll be remembered because its the sort of place where folk talk to each other. A colourful mix of customers, with regulars, tourists, lawyers, actors and musicians co-existing effortlessly.

Named after the nearby Victoria bridge, it has ridden on the crest of many waves of change. Even today as the Bridgegate accommodates a growth in "up-market" businesses and a new generation of wealthier residents, it is a bar which need not change its popular character. In its 60-year history, it has won awards for the quality of real ale, boasting Theakston's Best Bitter, Greenmantle & Merlin in addition to a quality pint of Murphy's or Guinness. An unusual stock of malts decorate the original wooden gantry. One concession to current trends is the availability of tea & coffee.

Live folk music is a regular occurence with spontaneous sing-a-long playing sessions as well as the monthly singers' workshop which provides a great alternative to Saturday afternoon shopping.

Hot (as opposed to Haute) cuisine for under £1 is recommended, in particular the Arbroath Pies and that unbeatable favourite - home made soup. A classic, class unconscious hostelry!

BETWEEN 1926 & 1938 DRINKING HOURS IN GLASGOW WERE 11AM - 3PM, 5PM - 9PM. SATURDAYS 10AM - NOON AND FROM 3PM - 9PM.

ZHIVAGO'S

178 Ingram Street

TEL: 552 0876

Dryboroughs, XXXX, Skol, Lowenbrau,

Bright neon signs, low slung grey velvet couches, large video screens, 70's silver legged glass topped tables (which are equally low) greet the drinker at Zhivago's. Frequented by well heeled D.H.S.S. and Glasgow District Council office workers at lunchtimes, and often groups of 40 of them or more when one of their number retires, gets promoted or celebrates a birthday.

At weekends a young disco crowd gathers, warming up for Zico's the basement disco which hosts amongst other theme nights, a divorced separated and singles night. A large mixed up pub which also houses a dining area and has old film posters framed on the walls. No natural daylight and the dim lighting add to the seediness of this city -centre pub, however, we are assured there is never any trouble at night. There are eight burly bouncers to get past at the front door and this might explain their claims that Zhivago's is young, lively and boisterous but trouble-free!

1. FINLAY'S
2. FLORIDA PARK
3. GRANARY
4. JEANIE
5. J.J. BOOTH'S
6. MAXWELL'S
7. MISSION
8. MULBERRY HOTEL
9. NAPOLEONS
10. OLD SMIDDY
11. OUTHOUSE
12. VILLAGE

RESTAURANTS

13. DI MAGGIO'S
14. GREEK GOLDEN KEBAB
15. MEHFIL

DARNLEY RD.
POLLOKSHAWS ROAD
VICTORIA RD.
QUEEN'S DRIVE
TITWOOD ROAD
QUEEN'S PARK
4
MINARD ROAD
DINMONT ROAD
MOSS-SIDE RD.
13
6
LANGSIDE AVE.
LANGSIDE ROAD
GRANGE RD.
CATHCART ROAD
3
POLLOKSHAWS ROAD
8
15
CAMPHILL AVENUE
MILLBRAE ROAD
14
SINCLAIR DRIVE
BATTLEFIELD ROAD
12
7
1
2
HOLMLEA ROAD
CATHCART RD.
11
KING'S PK. RD.
5
KINTORE RD.
KILMARNOCK ROAD
NETHERAULDHOUSE RD.
NEWLANDS ROAD
OLD CASTLE ROAD
DRIVE
MERRYLEE ROAD
9
10
CLARKSTON ROAD
LANGSIDE

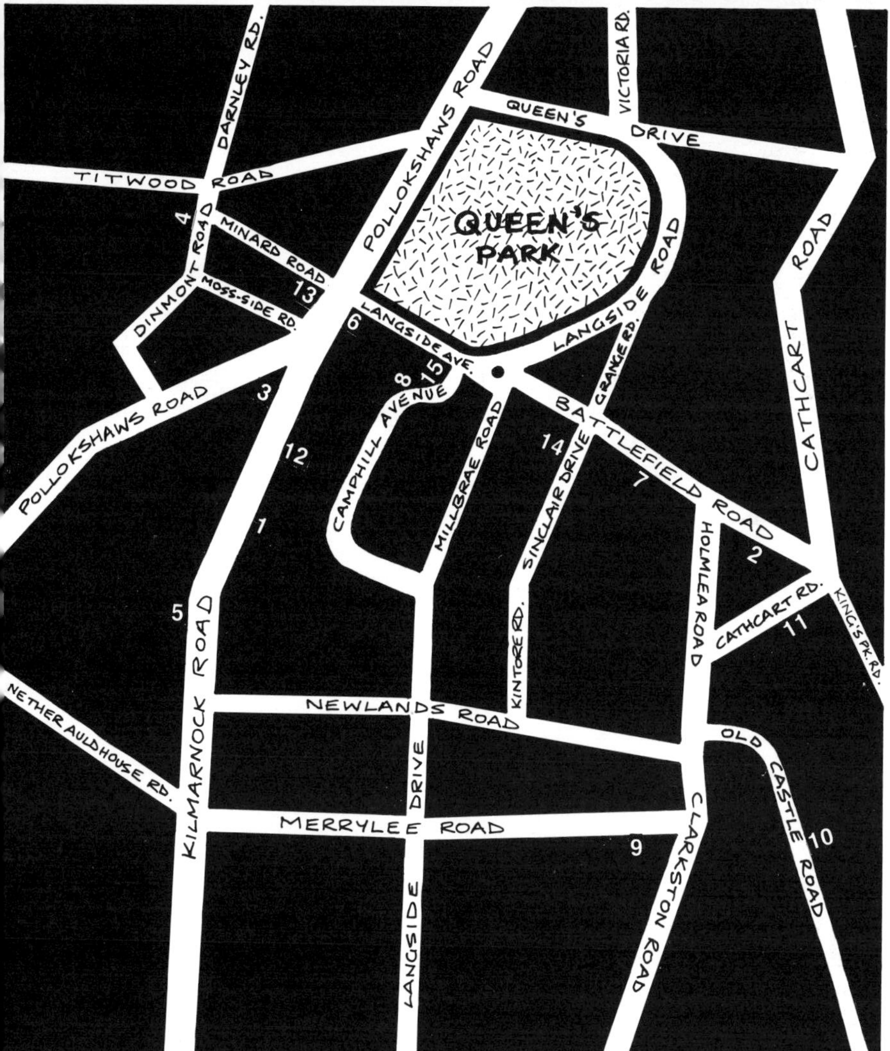

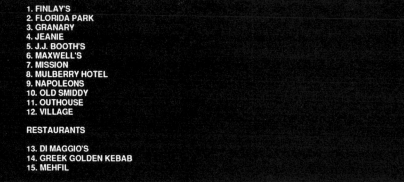

FINLAY'S

137/139 Kilmarnock Road

TEL: 632 0029

Tennent's Beers.

A lively pub, frequented by local south siders in great numbers, which creates a noisy, bustling atmosphere. On two levels, the bar can accommodate around 200 people, although on a Friday night you get the impression that it's nearer 300. With hessian wall paper and other dated features, its hard to see the attraction of this pub. The rear of the bar houses approximately six, small, very cosy drinking booths that encourage snogging and other familiar and trivial pursuits. The bar is also host to regular drink promotion and general knowledge quiz evenings, with a young chart music minded clientele, so - the attraction, whatever else it is, is very potent!

FLORIDA PARK

318 Battlefield Road

TEL: 649 9757

Tennent's Beers.

You could be mistaken for thinking you were having a drink in someone's livingroom. Airbrush 70's prints line the walls above brown velour couches & booths. A carpeted bar with a warm atmosphere, aided by coloured spot lights. Very much a seating bar, with very little room to stand, waitress service is available.

Regulars are middle aged couples who enjoy a quiz of an evening. Same emphasis on fun as most south-side bars, but attracting a more mature or shall we say older clientele. In addition to the regular general knowledge quiz evenings, live music is on offer, Friday & Saturday nights.

Pub grub available from lunchtimes through until evenings, cooked on the premises. Average prices, average drinks, although a good cocktail list, including their very own "Florida Park": Brandy, Dark Creme de Cacao, Fresh Cream topped with Nutmeg & Cinnamon.

For all this, still a popular wee local for Mounties!

Florida Park
LOUNGE BAR DINER
Florida Park
LOUNGE BAR DINER
Phone 649 9757

IN 1889 CELTIC PLAYED THE UNITED ABSTAINERS (NAMED BECAUSE OF A STRONG BELIEF IN TEMPERANCE). CELTIC WON.

THE GRANARY

10 Kilmarnock Road

TEL: 632 8487/ 649 7769

Alloa 70/-, 80/-, Skol, XXXX, Lowenbrau, Burton, Arrol's.

s a former "regular" of Sammy Dow's, I was a mite concerned when the news came out that the old place was to be refurbished, however my concern was misplaced! The Granary has proven to be an excellent pub diner. The original decision to spend lavishly on the decor was a wise one, it looks as comfortable now as it did three years ago, with classy use of specially created colourful stained glass and wood. The child in me (and it seems everyone else) appreciates the constant motion of the model train which circuits one of the lounge bars close to ceiling height. The other main attraction being the real ale and exciting cocktails. It is difficult to resist the variety of food on offer throughout the day as it is reasonably priced and well presented. Many pubs have copied the Granary's style, particularly the raised galleries and memorabilia which line the walls, but few have achieved the character of the place and none have maintained the transformation over such a long period. Frequented by a well turned out clientele, where for a change, the bouncer at the door is not the best dressed.

THE JEANIE

6 Dinmont Road

TEL: 632 1064

Tennent's Beers.

Once known as Jean Armours, the Jeanie has no apparent connection with Rabbie Burns, but don't be put off by the facade of this bar, built on a gap site in Shawlands. Split into two areas there is a games room, housing pool tables, puggy machines and old photographs of famous sporting events. The main bar is a quiet lounge with a warm and welcoming atmosphere. Walls are adorned with specially commissioned McCormack drawings and historical photographs of Pollokshaws. With yet another contrast, there is a 60's, 70's and 80's juke box for those of us who can remember that era, and those who are hearing it for the first time. Upstairs is geared towards the younger, louder, livelier amongst us, aptly named the Metropolis Disco.

Guinness, expertly skimmed, is of such a consistency that you could almost write your name on the head. Light snacks, available throughout the day and meals, served between noon and 2.30 p.m., at ridiculously low prices, should satisfy most palates.

With particularly helpful staff, spotlessly clean surroundings and the ability to cater for so many different age groups and preferences, the Jeanie is an unusual local worth investigating.

J.J. BOOTH'S

290 Kilmarnock Road

TEL: 632 9171

McEwan's.

Part of the long established Newlands Hotel, J.J. Booth's was recently renovated. The investment has certainly paid off. A traditional decor of leather chesterfield chairs and couches, original mahogany fireplaces on two galleries and beautiful stone floors. Barrels and kegs acting as tables surround the large bar. Ceiling beams detail the range of drinks and food available.

With Shawlands fast becoming "Sin City of the South", the emphasis is on fun!, enticing the young clientele to drape themselves in streamers and Furstenberg flags whilst taking part in quiz games. This party atmosphere is definitely reminiscent of a Club 18-30's holiday (not that the authors would ever admit to having been on a Club 18-30 holiday!). A D.J. is in residence seven nights a week and there is live music on Tuesdays and Wednesdays. Every night in J.J. Booth's is different with adult X-rated trivia and soul nights.

MAXWELL'S

1041 Pollokshaws Road

TEL: 632 9028

Tennent's Beers.

A large, uninspiring pub. Fur nished in wall length dark brown velour couches with cream wall lights and mirrors. Frequented by all types from middle-aged married couples to the very young.

Service is quick and efficient - it needs to be to cater for the crowds. The attached Bloomsbury Square restaurant offers a range of Pizza, Pasta, Fish, Chicken and Steak dishes. Although a little pricier than you would expect, the food is fresh & appetising!

Smart pinstripe suited bouncers at the door make sure that the clientele isn't too young! Stakis, who own Maxwell's, are about to take over the adjacent Corona Bar, which must be one of the last bastions of the working man who wants to enjoy a beer in unpretentious surroundings. The two bars are to be amalgamated, making Maxwell's even larger than it already is! Currently you can enter from Langside Avenue or Pollokshaws Road, soon it will take up the entire corner.

Disco lights and revolving globes complement the disco and chart music played loudly on the P.A., although midweek the music is not too loud to diminish conversation. The usual Stakis standard of pub grub is available at lunchtime.

Maxwells is notable for its undistinguished features and lack of quiz night fun. Various sporting trophies behind the bar suggest that this is someone's local. Very popular at weekends.

THE WORLD'S FIRST PIPE BAND FORMED IN GOVAN IN 1882, STILL EXISTS TODAY, KNOWN AS THE SRATHCLYDE POLICE BAND.

THE MISSION

162 Battlefield Road

TEL: 649 7818

Campbell's 70/-, Heineken, Stella.

Much of the south-side of Glasgow has traditionally been a "dry area", particularly in Mount Florida, Cathcart and Battlefield. The last few years have witnessed the emergence of four public houses in this alcoholic desert, the most recent being the Mission. One of the main attractions of this pub is the staff who manage to retain a friendly atmosphere, similar to a traditional "local pub" - although the Mission is bigger and better furnished than a typical "local".

The prices for spirits and their extensive range of lagers and foreign beers are extreemly good value. It's one of the few establishments which also serves coffee, tea and milk.

The pub is most popular with the 21 - 35 year olds, particularly between 2.30 and 7pm when the "happy hours" operate. A D.J. can often be found at night playing the latest charts and hosting trivia competitions, which appear to be popular.

The decor, the food and the very fact that a decent local pub exists, make the Mission a proverbial "dessert" in this particular desert!

A 'HALF & A HALF' WAS INVENTED BY AN IRISHMAN IN GLASGOW IN THE 18TH CENTURY.

MULBERRY HOTEL

2 Camphill Avenue

TEL: 632 9105

Tennent's beers.

Once owned by the proprietor of the famous Bon Accord in North Street and hence known for its selection of Real Ale, only the Tennent's 80/- remains. A fourteen bedroom hotel, with two distinctly different bars. As you enter choose either the public bar which has a more mature clientele and dark brown atmosphere or opt for the younger, trendier atmosphere of the lounge bar. A local D.J. holds court at weekends playing all of the latest chart-busters in the lounge. Decor is bright, pastel colours and air-brush flamingo prints break the monotony of the walls. Both bars have a strong lived-in feel about them and are most popular with nurses from the nearby Victoria Infirmary or students escaping from Langside College, as well as local customers.

Agreeably priced meals are available, contrasting with the style and quantity offered in the adjacent Mehfil Indian Restaurant next door.

NAPOLEONS

128 Merrylee Road

TEL: 637 5238

Tennent's Beers.

The only French feature found in Napoleons is the range of portraits at the rear of the bar. Nightly entertainment, flashlit dance floor, music quizzes, party nights and pop videos typify the character. Live performances by "up and coming" Glasgow bands are promoted once a month and the customers love it! The fairly well heeled custom can keep an eye on their cars from any part of this large, flashy bar, courtesy of a series of television screens relaying whatever might be happening in the car park, so if you are the type who tends to be paranoid about the safety of your motor vehicle, this facility will be attractive.

The former Bonaparts Restaurant (no spelling error here!) has been turned into a lounge, in an attempt to cater for a more mature clientele in this area which has very few pubs. Competing for the custom of the south-side thrill seekers, Napoleons has a round, well staffed bar surrounded by white wrought iron garden furniture. The more intimate gallery floor is quickly filled by those who arrive early enough, and as it is full to overflowing most evenings you would have to get there pretty early indeed. A very lively pub, evidenced by the array of photographs showing customers in a variety of embarrassing situations, however in order to view these photographs you have to get past the "burly bouncers". The policy is smart dress and trouble-free, so wear your best!

An Italian/State-side type menu is available throughout the day at average prices. In summary, unless you are fun-loving, don't mind crowds and want a great, unpredictable night out, the verdict on Napoleons has to be "not tonight Josephine".

OLD SMIDDY

131 Old Castle Road

TEL: 633 1122

Alloa Beers.

Your traditional, unpretentious local. A basically furnished bar with original dark wood ceiling beams, good, sturdy, sensibly sized tables, the occasional real plant and old prints. The kind of pub that doesn't need to justify itself. Dim wall lights add to the cosy, intimate feel of the place and you can see from the various pewter, brass and stainless steel tankards which hang behind the bar that there are many regulars whose association with the Smiddy goes back a long way. The television only goes on for particular programmes, for example Taggart is a must with the customers, but the volume is such that it needn't interfere with intense conversations taking place in small pockets.

Previously well known for the quality of the pub grub, the small portions and current lack of regard to quality are a disappointment, although the cost is very low indeed. The evening populace in the lounge is mainly older couples, whilst the bar is dominated by " the men", presided over by "Happy Harry", your original, head in the sand, grumpy and grudging manager. The rest of the staff with their pleasant manner, often over compensate for "Happy Harry's" unjustifiably abrupt and aggressive behaviour.

THE OUTHOUSE

1155 Cathcart Road

TEL: 649 0184

Tartan Special, McEwan's 80/-, Beck's, Harp.

Opened in '86, the Outhouse revitalised south-side drinking, encouraging many locals to save the taxi fare into town.

With the decor and atmosphere previously only found in the west-end the Outhouse has attracted custom from throughout the city. Tastefully decorated with hessian ceiling drapes, Stephen Campbell paintings, a large wooden/stained glass bar and stone floor. A feature is the living flame open fire, a strong attraction on cold winter evenings. Established by the owners of the Cul de Sac the bar has now been taken over by Scottish & Newcastle who have plans to refurbish as custom has been dwindling fast.

The once popular restaurant has now been limited to lunchtimes and weekend evenings offering moderately priced pizzas and pasta dishes. A resident D.J. has also been brought in to attract younger locals. Still a pleasant enough pub to enjoy a few drinks in and who knows what the proposed refurbishment will bring.

THE VILLAGE

61 Kilmarnock Road

TEL: 649 2745

Tennent's Beers.

Definitely the place to be seen if you are young and keen to meet new people. This incredibly popular Stakis Fun Palace plays host to regular drink promotions, lovely legs competitions and D.J. Quiz nights. The decor is certainly an original concept, unlikely to be copied elsewhere. Green plastic vines and cane seating screams at you as you enter, followed by a fake village terrace at the rear - a rather pretentious representation of an English country village. A mock antiquarian Bookshop, Teashop, Bakery, Haberdashery complete with white imitation fluffy clouds surround the terrace which itself is furnished with white wrought iron garden furniture and coca-cola parasols!

The "Rosie O'Grady" function room, downstairs, is available for private parties, and standard pub grub of Steak Pie, Chilli, Pizza and Lasagne are on offer between 12 noon and 5 pm. Always mobbed at the week-end. Having a drink here can ensure hours of entertainment, whether taking part in the frivolity or just watching!

THE GLASGOW

FOR THE QUESTION - SEE PAGE 4.

ANSWERS

BALGRAYHILL
BARNHILL
BLACKHILL
BLAWARTHILL
BROOMHILL
CAMPHILL
CLINCARTHILL
COPLAWHILL
CRANHILL
CRANSTONHILL
CROSSHILL
DOVEHILL
DOWANHILL
DUNDASHILL
FERNHILL
FIRHILL
GADSHILL
GARNETHILL
GILMOREHILL
GOVANHILL
HAGHILL
HAMILTONHILL
HOLEHILL
JORDANHILL
KEPPOCHHILL
LAMBHILL
LANGSIDEHILL
LETHAMHILL
LITTLEHILL
MARYHILL
NITSHILL
PARTICKHILL
PETERSHILL
PROSPECTHILL
PRIESTHILL
ROYSTONHILL
RUCHILL
SCOTSTOUNHILL
SIGHTHILL
SIMSHILL
STOBHILL
SUMMERHILL
WHITEHILL
YORKHILL

THE GLASGOW PUB & RESTAURANT GUIDE

by

Sandra Wilson, Sheila Adamson
& Allan Hutcheon.

£3.45

A Guide to Over 100 Pubs & Restaurants

POLYGON BOOKS

First published by
Polygon
22 George Square, Edinburgh

Printed in Great Britain by
Bell & Bain Ltd
Glasgow

British Library Cataloguing
in Publication Data
Wilson, Sandra
The Glasgow pub and restaurant guide.
1. Scotland. Strathclyde Region. Glasgow.
Public houses—Visitors guides
2. Scotland. Restaurant
I. Title II. Adamson, Sheila III. Hutcheon, Allan
647.'9541443

ISBN 0 948275 57 X

THE GLASGOW PUB & RESTAURANT GUIDE

Authors: Sandra Wilson, Sheila Adamson, Allan Hutcheon.

Hingers On: Robin Taggart, Mikey McCormick, Owen, Neil, Phil Armes & Pat Urquhart.

Cover Illustration By: Rosamund Fowler
Photography By: Paula Carley
Additional Photographs By: Sandra Wilson
Maps & Symbols by: Janice Taylor

Typeset & Designed on Apricot Computer by:
Sandra Wilson & Sheila Adamson.

Special Thanks To: The library assistants at the Mitchell Library.

Real Ale

Meals **Puggy Machines**

Live Music **T.V.**

Condom Machine

Sunday Opening

TRON *EFFECTIVE DIRECT* MARKETING

THE GLASGOW

CONTENTS

2

THE GLASGOW

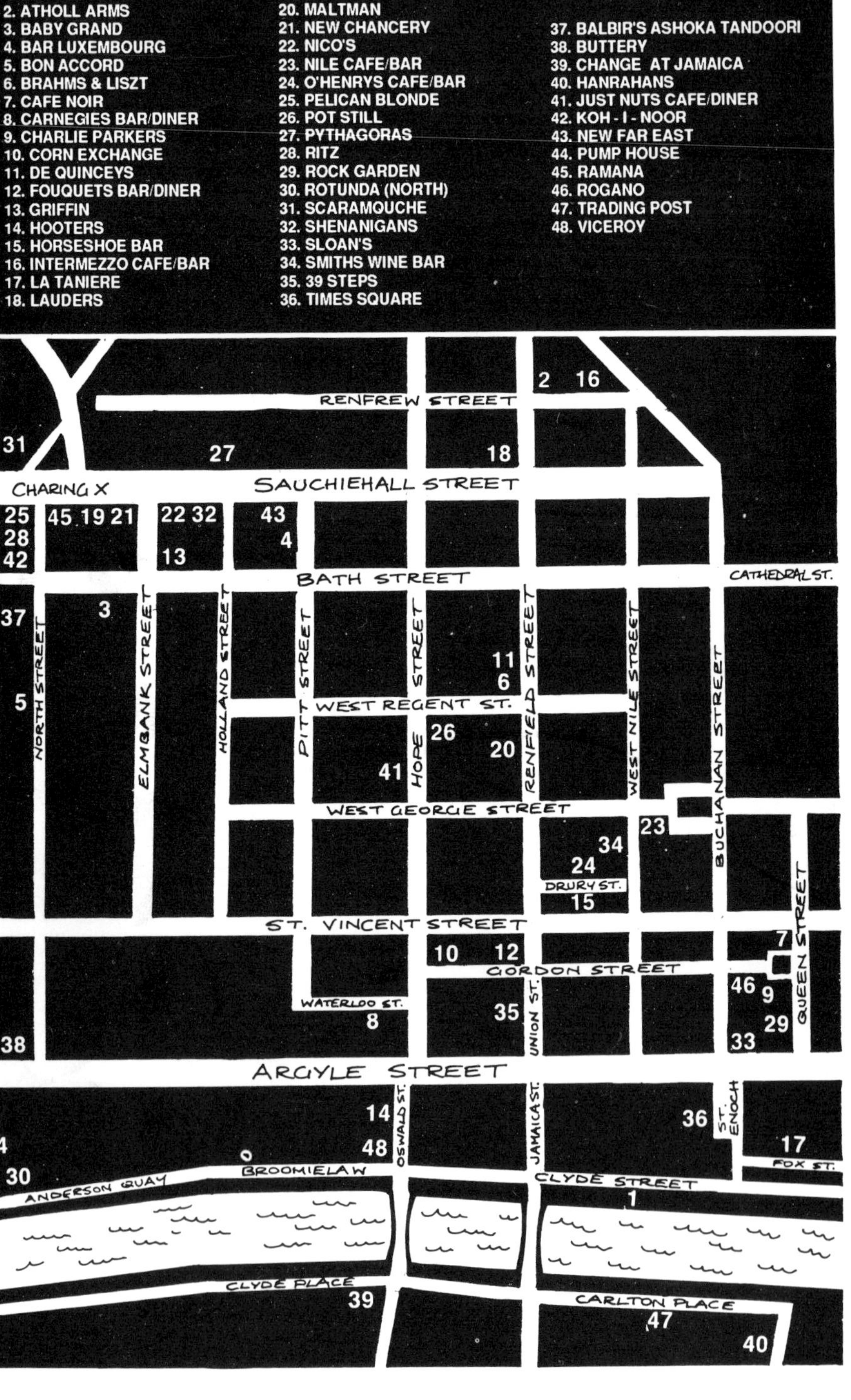
1. ADVOCATE
2. ATHOLL ARMS
3. BABY GRAND
4. BAR LUXEMBOURG
5. BON ACCORD
6. BRAHMS & LISZT
7. CAFE NOIR
8. CARNEGIES BAR/DINER
9. CHARLIE PARKERS
10. CORN EXCHANGE
11. DE QUINCEYS
12. FOUQUETS BAR/DINER
13. GRIFFIN
14. HOOTERS
15. HORSESHOE BAR
16. INTERMEZZO CAFE/BAR
17. LA TANIERE
18. LAUDERS
19. L'ODEON CAFE/BAR
20. MALTMAN
21. NEW CHANCERY
22. NICO'S
23. NILE CAFE/BAR
24. O'HENRYS CAFE/BAR
25. PELICAN BLONDE
26. POT STILL
27. PYTHAGORAS
28. RITZ
29. ROCK GARDEN
30. ROTUNDA (NORTH)
31. SCARAMOUCHE
32. SHENANIGANS
33. SLOAN'S
34. SMITHS WINE BAR
35. 39 STEPS
36. TIMES SQUARE
RESTAURANTS
37. BALBIR'S ASHOKA TANDOORI
38. BUTTERY
39. CHANGE AT JAMAICA
40. HANRAHANS
41. JUST NUTS CAFE/DINER
42. KOH - I - NOOR
43. NEW FAR EAST
44. PUMP HOUSE
45. RAMANA
46. ROGANO
47. TRADING POST
48. VICEROY
RENFREW STREET
CHARING X
SAUCHIEHALL STREET
BATH STREET
CATHEDRAL ST.
NORTH STREET
ELMBANK STREET
HOLLAND STREET
PITT STREET
HOPE STREET
RENFIELD STREET
WEST NILE STREET
BUCHANAN STREET
WEST REGENT ST.
WEST GEORGE STREET
DRURY ST.
ST. VINCENT STREET
GORDON STREET
WATERLOO ST.
UNION ST.
QUEEN STREET
ARGYLE STREET
OSWALD ST.
JAMAICA ST.
ST. ENOCH
FOX ST.
BROOMIELAW
ANDERSON QUAY
CLYDE STREET
CLYDE PLACE
CARLTON PLACE

RESTAURANT GUIDE

DANNY BROWN'S (NOW CASKIES) HIGH TEAS OF SOLE, CHIPS, LAMB CHOPS, BACON, EGGS, TEA & TOAST COST 2S 9D IN 1939.

BALBIR'S ASHOKA TANDOORI
108 Elderslie Street

TEL: 221 1761

MON-SAT 12 NOON - 12 MIDNIGHT
SUNDAY 5PM - 12 MIDNIGHT

Rumoured to be one of the best Indian restaurants in the city. Upstairs and down this restaurant can accommodate over 100 diners. A welcome and informative menu enlightens those of us who are unfamiliar with or even confused by the culinary terms which prevail. The menu clearly details the ingredients of each dish ranging from Makhani Massala prepared by cooking ground Nuts and Tomatoes with Massala in butter, with a generous amount of cream, to Leg of Lamb Shahi Massalum, a feast for 4 people. Located in Elderslie Street, it is a little off the beaten track, but worth checking out.

Assuming that the food remains of a high quality, the Ashoka reputation should continue to be first class as staff go out of their way to ensure satisfaction. The Ashoka should not just be left until after the pubs shut, it is ideal for an enjoyable meal and evening out.

There is no connection between Balbir's Ashoka and the Ashoka (west end).

THE FIRST REGISTERED TEA ROOM IN LONDON WAS STARTED BY A SCOTSMAN, ROBERT MCDOUGALL IN 1876.

BUTTERY
652 Argyle Street

TEL: 221 8188

MON - SAT: 12 NOON - 3 PM;
7 PM - 11 PM.

Housed on the ground floor of a typical Glasgow tenement, surrounded by a variety of derelict sites, ugly 60's housing and the motorway, you will find on of Glasgow's most famous and exclusive restaurants. The facade and location suggest the existence of a level of inverted snobbery which is more in evidence as Glasgow's public face changes. Some would say that good food generates success despite such surroundings and there is no doubt that the Buttery cuisine is of a very high standard.

On entering, the calm order of Victoriana is instantly recognisable. Courteous, discret, but distant service is provided by staff bedecked in "Upstairs, Downstairs" regalia, which is entirely in keeping with the carefully recreated Victorian decor.

A place to visit for very special occasions, unless you are in the habit of spending a lot of money on food, and should you be anxious to avoid embarrassment don't try to order a bottle of Piesporter Michelsberg - they no longer stock it, reflecting their increasingly up-market and very costly stock.
The menu is magnificent, although I rarely resist opting for the Venison. If you don't have the appetite for a full meal you could indulge in some fresh salmon, served at the bar - very decadent!

The normal clientele are confidently comfortable with the "silver service" approach to every aspect of the Buttery, but some might be a little intimidated by the mop-capped staff who sweep the table at regular intervals with their silver brush and shovel!

Downstairs, a much more casual approach prevails in the Belfry Bar. An ideal location to meet friends for a quiet chat.

"BALL" ALLAN WAS KNOWN AS THE CANDY KING OF GLASGOW. HIS SHOP WAS ON THE EAST SIDE OF CROWN STREET.

CHANGE AT JAMAICA
7 Clyde Place

TEL: 429 4422

MON-WED 12 NOON- 12 MIDNIGHT
THURS 12 NOON - 2AM
FRI/SAT 12 NOON - 6AM
SUN 6 PM - 12 MIDNIGHT

Transformed from the railway arches into a striking black & white art deco restaurant. When did you last see a train come through the wall! The restaurant is very much a designer concept, with black & white tiled floor, glass tables with linen table cloths, designer mirrors and chairs, and even a Sapporo Japanese designer lager on offer! A varied menu that would make your mouth water, which draws on French, Italian and British cuisine for its inspiration.
Some very original dishes such as Jamaican Fillet, served with Jamaican Butter and Wild Woodland Mushrooms or Sole Yellowman, Gougons of Lemon Sole and Banana, crumbled and shallow fried in lemon and butter.To wash down your meal there is an impressive wine list, even stretching to Australian wines. Draught Stella, Heineken, and a good range of foreign bottled and canned beers are also in stock. The music is loud enough to cover the noise of the trains overhead, and is a mixture of everything from Classical to Hip Hop. Despite this, there is a relaxed atmosphere and the service is quick and courteous.

HANRAHANS
16 Nicholson Street

TEL: 420 1069

MON - SAT 11AM - 11PM
SUN 7PM - 11PM

The look is refined................ Hanrahans has already taken Glasgow's lunchtime and night-time cognoscenti by storm...... sophisticated ambience......it is undoubtedly one of the best restaurants in Glasgow......the ultimate place for those who expect and enjoy excellence in their lifestyle". Having read these and many similar quotes, I arrived at Hanrahans with high expectations...... and was not disappointed!. The advertising claims are not only substantiated, but exceeded.

THE FAMOUS "COULTERS CANDY" SONG WAS WRITTEN BY A MAN NAMED COULTART, WHO DIED IN 1890.

Opened only in January, '88, this three-storey, compact building has been transformed from a long-term derelict tenement into a plush restaurant. The design is strong, suggesting all that was attractive in the best "Victorian Gentleman's Club", minus the sexism! Restaurants of this calibre with such opulent surroundings can be in danger of intimidating the clientele, however, this possibility has been eradicated through a careful choice of staff. Their warmth and straightforward ability to communicate comfortably with patrons is instantly conveyed. Evidence of a subtle sense of humour can be found in the (almost illegible) latin motto which translates as "five Woodbines and a fish supper"!

Hanrahans has an unconfirmed history involving the birth of one James Hanrahan on the premises. James apparently crossed the Atlantic, became a Tobacco Lord, and upon his return to Glasgow, embarked upon a legal career.

The absence of any empirical evidence supporting this is quite unimportant. What does matter is the impressive variety of beverages and the menus, all designed to give the customer what s/he wants; when s/he wants it and at a price which should embarrass some of Glasgow's longer-established quality restaurants.

Recommended dishes include Roast Beef, from the lunchtime menu and Grilled Minute Steak Garni, from the Business Luncheon Menu, which at under £5 for 2 courses and coffee is staggering value. My favourite is the Pre-Theatre Menu, available between 6-7.30p.m., when £7.50 will buy you a 3 course meal. I indulged in Pavarotti's Downfall, the Nutcracker and "finished off" with Swan Lake. The Table d'Hote Menu, at £14.25 is in the same Scottish, with a strong French influence, category.

A meal at Hanrahans is a must for the "cognoscenti " - defined in the dictionary as "people with informed appreciation". You have been reliably informed!

IN 1923 THERE WAS A COIN CHIP MACHINE UNDER THE STOCKWELL STREET BRIDGE. A BAG OF HOT CHIPS COST SIXPENCE.

JUST NUTS CAFE/ DINER
201 Hope Street

TEL: 332 1469

MON - WED 11AM - 10PM
THURS/FRI/SAT 11AM - 11PM

This cafe/diner attached to Reids Bar has been open since 1986, although Reids itself has occupied this site for 25 years. Rumoured to be one of the first establishments in Glasgow to serve up mince pies and mushy peas!

There are no bones about it - Just Nuts offers a vast selection of filleted meats, accompanied by a choice of eight tempting sauces and if that's not enough you can even have a

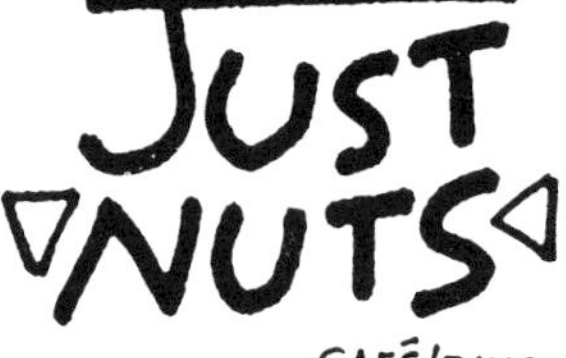

warm salad!

The menu is so varied it is hard to put it into a definite category, ranging from a selection of crepes and kebabs to stuffed croissants, burgers, pastas and steaks.

The biggest attraction has to be the reasonably priced wine list, with over 40 different wines from as little as £4.45 a bottle. Like the menu the decor is difficult to classify, however, the pale blue pastel shades and the friendly staff create a relaxed and comfortable atmosphere.

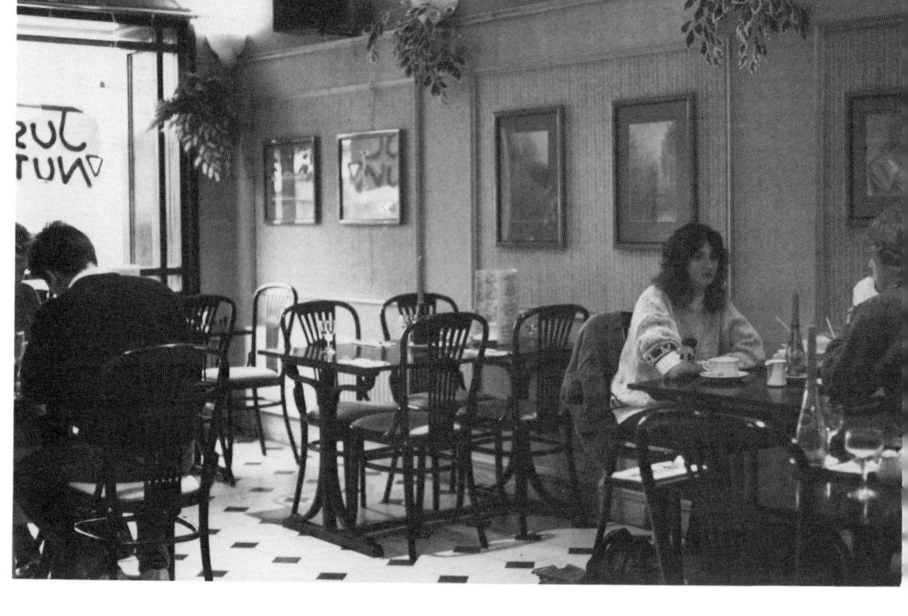

KOH-I-NOOR INDIAN RESTAURANT
235 North Street

TEL: 204 1444

MON-THU 12 NOON- 12 MIDNIGHT
FRI/SAT 12 NOON - 1AM
SUN 12 NOON - 12 MIDNIGHT

Any visitor or Glasgow food enthusiast should not miss out the Koh-I-Noor, surely one of Glasgow's finest curry houses. No gourmet of Indian cuisine could leave this establishment unsatisfied. The restaurant is huge, resulting in a situation which is never overcrowded or overbearing. Management do not try to compete with newer Indian restaurants, trying to be "modern", satisfying itself and its customers with authentic, quality food. No bright lights and flashy music here - just eastern atmosphere and superb cuisine served in large portions at very reasonable prices.

The menu covers most aspects of Indian cooking you'll have heard of and some which you won't have heard of before. The special dishes represent extemely good value for money.

A full bar facility is available in addition to a small lounge. If you haven't tried the Koh-I-Noor, try it now - you won't beat it for quality, enhanced by the service from waiters who are discreet but attentive. Full marks!

IN THE REIGN OF KING JAMES I SAWNEY BEANE AND HIS FAMILY OF CANNIBALS LIVED IN CAVES NEAR GIRVAN.

NEW FAR EAST
303 Sauchiehall Street

TEL: 332 5737

MON-THU 12 NOON-2PM; 5-11.30;
FRI - SAT 12 NOON-12 MIDNIGHT;
SUN 5-11.30PM

If you don't ask, you don't get! This Cantonese restaurant is divided in two with a separate menu for each section - the pink menu, available in the back room, is not what you would expect from most "Anglicised Chinese restaurants", nor are the portions! Authentic Cantonese food , generous portions too! You always know that you've made the right choice when you see Chinese people dining at the next table - this is definitely the case in the New Far East. Eating such beautifully cooked food with a knife and fork always makes me feel a little guilty, so much so that I inevitably give into the temptation to have yet another attempt to use the chopsticks. The standard menu, which you will automatically be offered, includes King Prawn with Ginger and Spicy Onions, Chicken with Cashew Nuts and Pineapple and Yeung Chow Fried Rice. Whether you eat in or take-away, the prices represent unbelievably good value for money.
Remember to make a point of asking for the pink menu as it is not actively publicised or promoted by staff - you will not be disappointed!

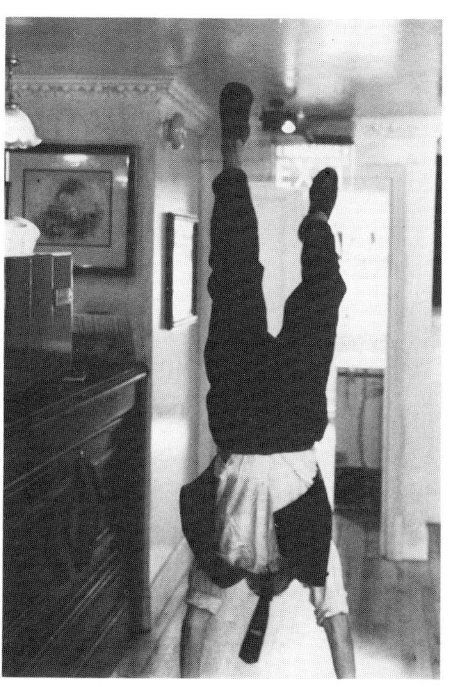

THE PUMP HOUSE
100 Stobcross Road

TEL: 221 5222

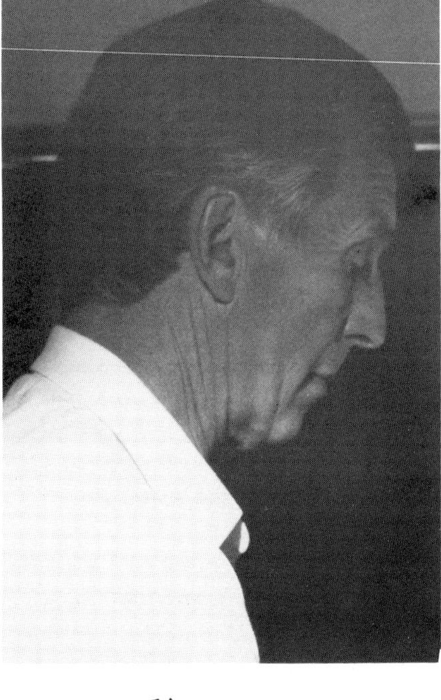

Formerly a working pump-house, this characterful sandstone building sitting on the edge of the river has been transformed at a staggering cost of over £2M! Housing 3 dynamically different restaurants, designed to suit those among us whose willingness to spend substantial sums of money in return for magnificent surroundings and up-market menus.

Overlooking the river, the Rusty Pelican Fish and Grill Conservatory offers every conceivable type and style of seafood, whilst the neighbouring Little Venice Ristorante Italiano menu is of a more conservative nature. The third aspect of this novel concept is the Bombay Club - not what you would describe as a curry-house - where again the emphasis is on more adventurous cuisine, encompassing unusual seafood with an Indian treatment.

It is possible that you will be so stunned by the opulence and grandeur of your surroundings, (particularly the Bombay Club) that the quality and cost of your meal will go relatively unnoticed. I indulged in the Pate Della Casa, Ossobuca alla Milanese and Zabaglione. The Pate was excellent, the veal disappointing and, I suspect, the Zabaglione was really marshmallow, thinly disguised. It is true that my luck hasn't been all good recently and perhaps I chose unwisely. Whatever the explanation, the cost of a meal in Little Venice leads me to expect more in respect of concern for the diner's enjoyment than was forthcoming. I will return to try the Bombay Club.

THE HEAVIEST MAN IN GLASGOW WAS WILLIAM CAMPBELL, BORN 1852, DIED 1872 WEIGHING 52 STS AND 6FT 3IN IN HEIGHT

RESTAURANT RAMANA
427 Sauchiehall Street

TEL: 332 2528/ 2590

MON-THU 12 NOON-12 MIDNIGHT
FRI - SAT 12 NOON - 1AM
SUN 2PM - 12 MIDNIGHT

Named after the Hindu God of Food, Restaurant Ramana was the first Indian restaurant in Sauchiehall Street to feature Tandoori cooking. Opened in '76 it has undergone constant decorative improvements, subtly reflecting the increased expectations of diners. Subtlety is a key feature of the extensive menus, concentrating on real Delhi cooking methods which exercise the same restraint associated with classical European dishes.

The main menu details 86 Indian and 14 European dishes as well as the more usual accompaniments. Past customers include Dave Allen and the Indian High Commissioner, although I understand that they didn't share a table!

Of particular note are the Korma dishes. Choose the rich, creamy Shahi Korma, the fruitier Kashmiri Korma, the Ceylonese style or the Exotic Madrasi, combining yogurt and ground Channa. The star of the Korma range has to be the Dilbaliar, with the gourmet blend of Cream & Cashew Nuts. Also offering a childrens' menu and a variety of business lunches, the menu to be sure to try is the Gourmet Buffet. Available between 6 - 10pm Sundays - Wednesdays, select your own three course meal - astonishing value!

An integral lounge bar, frequented by a younger clientele, serves up the usual range of beverages at lower than average prices, also available to diners. However, if you seek something special to drink, complement the quality food by indulging in a bottle of Indian Champagne!

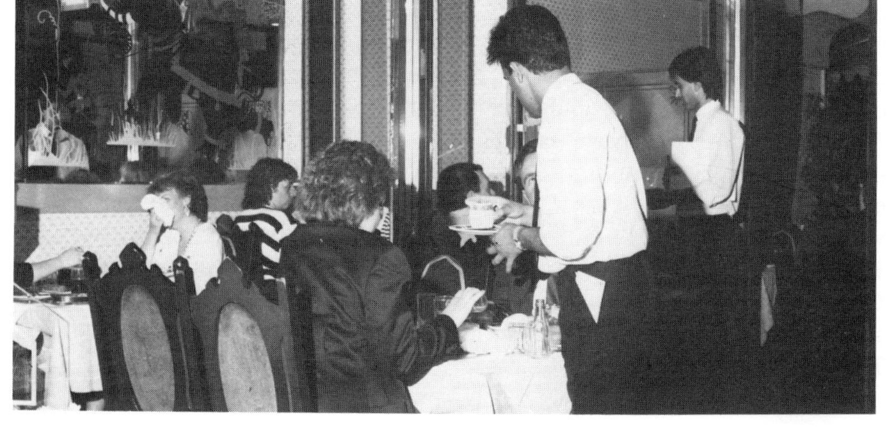

GLASGOW ARTIST C. BAILLIE'S FAMOUS MURAL OF APHRODITE RISING FROM THE SEA CAN BE SEEN IN THE ROGANO.

ROGANO
11 Exchange Place

TEL: 248 4055

MON - THURS 12 NOON - 11PM
FRI - SAT 12 NOON - 12 MIDNIGHT

First established in 1876, the Rogano still flourishes today. It has seen, and survived the desperate poverty of the city. Renowned for its similarity in decor to the famous Clyde built liner, the Queen Mary, with magnificent wood panelling; Aphrodite rising from the sea; ornate tiling and plain unspoilt class, the main restaurant deserves its reputation. Specialising in seafood but also offering meat and vegetarian dishes, lunch will cost around £25 and an evening meal £32 on average.

The recently opened Cafe Rogano, in the basement, continues the 30's "art-deco" style, but is less formal. Wonderful framed black and white photographs of famous people, complete with famous quotes, use up the wall space in an amusing, interesting way. A life-size "art-deco" female relentlessly holds her illuminated globe skyward, but the most impressive fact of all is that an excellent dinner for two, including wine will cost around £25. The Brasserie type menu is less traditional than upstairs, introducing slightly more adventurous dishes. Typically lunch here will cost around £8.50 and the attractive Oyster Bar lunch at approximately £5 means that the Rogano is a particularly busy lunch venue.

I am pleased to note that as the years have passed, Rogano quality has remained indisputable and the value, in real terms, has improved. Comparison with other "quality" restaurants in the city, where dinner for two costs around £70 leaves no doubt that this is the case. Excellent service from well trained staff and an air of romantic nostalgia make this the perfect venue for important occasions.

THE ADVOCATE

GLASGOW'S ONLY WATERFRONT PUB

CUSTOMS HOUSE QUAY GARDENS
OFF CLYDE STREET, GLASGOW.
(Below the Suspension Bridge)
TELEPHONE: 041-221 0021

PANAMA JA
GLASGOW'S
Nº 1
DISCO

CUSTOM HOUSE QUAY GARDE
GLASGOW
TEL: DAY 041-429 6308 NIGHT 041-221

TRADING POST
AUTHENTIC AMERICAN
BAR & STEAKHOUSE

63, CARLTON PLACE. TEL. 041-429 3445
GLASGOW

'Good ole frontier hospitality'

GLASGOW'S MOST ORIGINAL
SALOON BAR
WESTERN DECOR
MANY U.S.A. & FOREIGN BEERS
BAR VITTALS

B-B-Q
YOUR OWN
AT OUR
UNIQUE AMERICAN
FRONTIER RESTAURANT

LATE LICENCE
MONDAY - FRIDAY
OPEN TO 1 A.M.

BUSINESS LUNCH
£3·50
MONDAY TO FRIDAY
HIGH NOON - 2.30 P.M.

McFARLANE
GROUP OF COMPANIES

THE HOLIDAY INN HOTEL
ARGYLE ST.
CENTRAL STATION.
BUCHANAN S
ST. ENOCH BUS STATION + TUBE STATION
TO S.E.C.
BROOMIELAW.
M8
RIVER CLYDE.
DEVILS ADVOC AND PANAMA NIGHTCLUB
CLYDE ST.
RIVER CLYDE
TRADING POST
HANRAHANS

HANRAHANS
AT NICHOLSON STREET

Restaurant & Lounge Bar

PRE THEATRE MENU
TABLE D'HOTE MENU

GREEN ROOM
Restaurant
NOW OPEN ALL DAY
Mon-Sat 11 a.m.-11 p.m.
Sunday 7 p.m.-11 p.m.

BUSINE LUNCH
Daily
12 noon-2.3
£4.75

JUDGE THE QUALITY FOR YOURSELF
16 NICHOLSON STREET
TEL. 041-420 1069
Directly Opposite New Sheriffs Court

THE TRADING POST
63 Carlton Place

TEL: 429 3445

MON - SAT 12 NOON - 2.30PM;
6PM - 1AM;
SUN 7PM - 11PM

Ever felt like shooting the chef who's just presented you with a steak that is not your idea of medium rare? Ever wanted to investigate the kitchen, just to be sure that it is clean ?
If you recognise these emotions (guaranteed indigestion) mosey on down to this authentic American Bar and Steakhouse where you can cook your own meal, at your own table, to your own taste! Each table has an in-built gas fired barbeque, and if, like me, you can't cook, the Chef will cook for you.

As you would expect, this "good ole frontier" menu also offers Bunk House Breakfasts; the Great American Burger, Spaghetti Westerns and Hungry Jack's Pancakes, to name but a few. The prices compare well with other steakhouses and the kid's menu in particular is great value. They didn't have Desperate Dan Pie when I was wee!

This extreme theme bar goes further than any other to encourage a good belly laugh and a great belly full, but there are two things I should warn you about. You cannot make a sophisticated entrance, as you are liable to be shot on entry, so if you have a nervous disposition, don't say that you were not warned. Should the volley of rifle shots fail to put you in a Wild West mood, look out for the life-sized talking horse (it's really the barman talking), I guarantee that his humourous patter will raise a smile, at least.

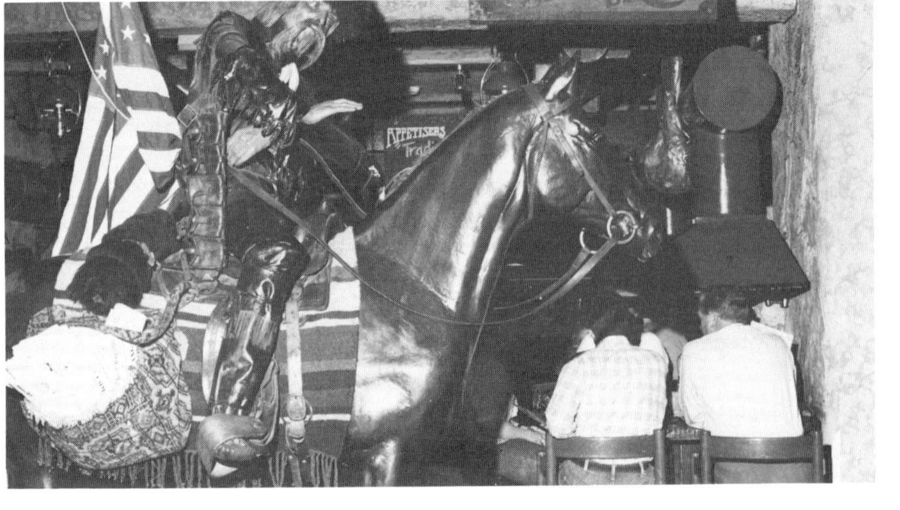

VICEROY
27 Oswald Street

TEL: 221 9339

MON - FRI 12 NOON - 12 MIDNIGHT
SAT 5PM - 12 MIDNIGHT

If it weren't for the Indian pictures which decorate the walls you could easily believe that this restaurant was European. The decor is quite different, strong gothic features, bamboo, cane furniture and ivy plants prevail. The toilets definitely merit a mention as what must be the cleanest in Glasgow. We are informed that reviewers come from miles around to photograph them.

The tandoori menu offers the whole gamut, Pakora, Spiced Popadoms, Chicken Passanda, the ubiquitous Mixed Thali for two, and Hins Tikka (venison). There is also an extensive European menu available for those not yet converted to the delights of Indian cuisine. Only opened in March '88, it is a little early to have gained a reputation one way or the other, however service is slick, and the waiters are keen to ensure that you enjoy your meal. I had the Hins Tikka as I adore venison and there aren't many places around that offer itwest end map cooked in this style, try it for yourself.

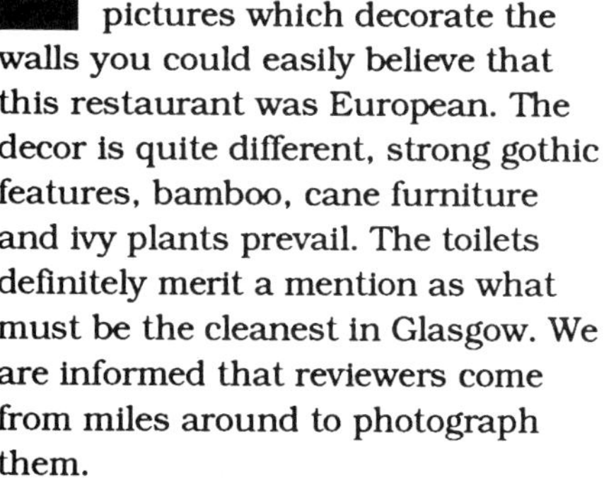

1. ARAGON
2. ARLINGTON BAR
3. BONHAMS
4. CHIMMY CHUNGAS
5. CUL DE SAC
6. CURLERS BAR
7. DIVA BAR/RESTAURANT
8. DOUBLET
9. EXCHEQUER BAR
10. FINLAY'S
11. HALT BAR
12. LA TAVERNA
13. LAUTREC'S BRASSERIE
14. OBLOMOV
15. O'HENRYS CAFE/BAR
16. REID'S OF PERTYCK
17. STIRLING CASTLE
18. STUDIO ONE
19. TENNENT'S

RESTAURANTS

20. ASHOKA WEST END
21. BACK ALLEY
22. BASIL'S VEGETARIAN CAFE
23. CREPERIE
24. DI MAGGIO'S
25. SPAGHETTI FACTORY
26. UBIQUITOUS CHIP

ASHOKA WEST END
1284 Argyle Street

TEL: 339 0936

7 days : 5PM - 1AM

A real problem presented itself to Gill, owner of the highly successful Ashoka. Its very success resulted in queues of expectant diners creating traffic jams at the door. Rather than extend the premises risking damage to the intimate cosiness which prevails, he bought both bars across the road. Instead of waiting in a long queue, you can now enjoy a leisurely drink and one of the chatty waiters will come to escort you across the road when your table is ready! A small, exclusively shabby restaurant seating around 25 upstairs and approximately 30 downstairs, staff need to be very fit and good humoured, constantly running back and forth across Argyle Street or balancing armfuls of beautifully presented food downstairs.

Ingenious place mats reproduce a glowing review of the premises by "Diner-Tec", and the Delhi Record, a four page newsheet typifies the gourmet blend of Glasgow culture and humour with Indian cuisine at its' best.

Divided into Gourmet, Tandoori and Popular sections, the menu concentrates on the Gourmet Section with Royal Massalums, cooked Punjabi style being the most salubrious dish featured - 3 hours notice is required. Chicken Tikka Chasni, will suit people with a delicate palate and the extremely popular Mix Thali for Two option lets you choose three dishes from the menu as well as starters at an incredible price. " The best vegetarian curries tasted in a long time!" was the verdict of a strictly vegetarian friend. Doggie bags are provided for those who haven't got huge appetites.

A unique curry house combining the best of Glasgow humour with the best in quality and quantity. A must for all curry connoisseurs.

THE LOON FUNG WAS THE DELUXE CINEMA. THE CINEMA CEILING IS PRESERVED IN THE MAIN PART OF THE RESTAURANT.

BACK ALLEY, Ruthven Lane

TEL: 334 7165

MON-THU 12 NOON - 2.30P ;
5 - 12 MIDNIGHT;
FRI 12 NOON - 2.30PM; 5 - 1 AM
SAT 12 NOON - 1 AM
SUN 5 - 12 MIDNIGHT

Part of the Mario and Renata Group of Restaurants, Back Alley specialises in Burgers, but also offers Steaks, Chicken, Fish and Filled Potato Skins.

Glazed common or garden bricks, cheered up by the presence of red tables and some classic film posters, prominently displayed, contribute to the civilised but casual aura.

There's some very serious eating goes on here. Choose from One-Eyed Jack - the "ace in the pack" burger stacked with cheese or tomato or try the "Too Hot toTrot" - yes, it is covered in a special Black Pepper Sauce. Half pounders for those who might find the more regular quarter pounder insufficient. The Thelma MacBreath (garlic bread) does exactly as it threatens, and the '49ers Chicken Nuggets are an unusual treatment of chicken.

Healthy portions (in size and health terms) - everything is accompanied by salad. Bottled Grolsch, cans of Schlitz, Stella, Pils and a choice of 5 house wines are on offer alongside the usual non-alcoholic beverages. Daily specials, eg. Chicken Suedoise, Chicken and Spinach Canneloni broaden the base menu. For those of us with a sweet tooth, try the Miami Ice - Vanilla Ice Cream/Hot Fudge Sauce locked in a Deep Fried Puff Pastry cell - like they say - decadence personified! Unusually the kids' and OAP's menu are one and the same thing. Popular with entire families up to 8pm. The special lunch menu is a real bargain.

Superbly cooked, presented with a sense of humour at prices that are far from hysterical.

THE LARGEST VINE IN THE WORLD WAS AT KIPPEN AND IT SPREAD ALL OVER A LARGE GLASSHOUSE.

BASIL'S VEGETARIAN CAFE
184 Dumbarton Road

TEL: 337 1416

WED - SAT 11AM - 9.30PM
SUNDAYS CLOSED
MONDAYS 11AM - 9.30PM
TUESDAYS 11AM - 2PM; 6.30 - 9.30PM

A great asset to the west-end, this recently opened cafe is the result of three years of effort by three ideologically-sound entrepreneurs. Edible proof that the co-operative principle can work, this Workers' Co-operative guarantees vegetarian/wholefood dishes, most of which are cooked on the premises, although they do confess to "buying-in" the oatcakes.

The menu is fairly limited with only five starters, 10 main courses and seven sweets to choose from, but that doesn't mean that you won't find choosing difficult. Of these, around half are suitable for vegans, eg, Nut Roast,celery, apple and cider roast served with miso gravy and a crunchy salad. Prices are very good - a three course meal shouldn't cost more than £6-7.

The decor is fresh and the use of muted colours strongly suggests vegetable dyes - a nice touch! A range of 12 fruit, herbal and oriental teas, including Pink Zinger or Mango, is offered in addition to organic coffee and, would you believe, organic wines! Yes, organic wines - choose the Chateau du Prade claret if looking for a fruity little number, or perhaps the medium dry Chateau Balluemondon. All very reasonably priced.

Maximum seating capacity is 40 and although Basil's is quite small,

tables are well spaced, allowing private conversation. Booking is advised in the evenings and at lunchtime on Fridays and Saturdays. A no smoking policy applies in part of the restaurant and, for me, this could have been a problem - I'm an addict! - however the taped 60's and 70's music nostalgically distracted me from thinking of my nicotine withdrawal symptomsand I could have sat in the smoking area.

The food, contrary to popular imagery of "rabbit food" is well presented and the result of an imaginative and extremely capable Chef's

efforts. The smoked Tofu and Leek Cocktail starter is recommended and their treatment of the baked potato merits a mention - Spud-de-Lux is overflowing with green peppers and mushrooms in a wine and mustard sauce, topped with sour cream of Greek yoghurt, served with another crunchy salad.

Vegetarians and non-vegetarians of all ages, types and sizes are to be found savouring this "menu with a difference" although it is fair to say that most fall within the 20-40 age range. Quarter gills of spirits are further evidence of the good value and Furstenberg, Grolsch, Red Stripe and Greenmantle are also available. You might prefer the Aspall organic still dry cider - too dry I'm sure to be related to Michael. A proverbial paradise for the growing number of vegetarians!

RAB HA' OR HAW WAS "THE GLESCA GLUTTON". HIS PROPER NAME WAS ROBERT HALL AND HE COULD OUT EAT ANYONE.

THE CREPERIE
Cul de Sac
44 Ashton Lane

TEL: 334 4749

MON - WED 12 NOON - 11.30PM
THURS - SAT 12 NOON - 12 MID-NIGHT
SUN 12 NOON - 11PM

Anything but a dead end, frequented by lots of theatricals and one of my favourites, the Creperie is a very modern eating house with strong art-nouveau features. A classy black and white tiled floor, equally classical pillars, an impressive art-deco statue and black wrought iron tables set the scene. Specially commissioned stained glass and Stephen Campbell originals complete the mood. Housed in what was Barr and Stroud's engineering factory, famed for the production of high quality lenses and opticals, many of the original characteristics still remain. The menu is based on a variety of crepes, fillings on offer include Spinach Gruyere, Honey Roast Ham, Cheese and Pineapple and of course Croque Monsieur. Pasta, Open Sandwiches and a selected wine list, bottled beers, coffees and sweets will tempt you into over indulgence. Tables are candlelit and the lights are dimmed in the evening creating a sophisticated, civilised yet casual ambience. At weekends diners are serenaded by musicians, sometimes on the piano, guitar or even playing the accordian. Jazz and classical pieces are normally associated with the Creperie.

Keep an eye open for the accordian player who was in "Tutti-Frutti", although you will spot quite a number of "stars" enjoying themselves of screen and stage. Located next door to the Grosvenor Cinema, meals are relatively inexpensive and of exceptional quality. A wonderful place to recharge your batteries and feed your digestive system simultaneously.

23

RESTAURANT GUIDE

THE BIGGEST CHEESE WAREHOUSE IN GLASGOW WAS IN BELL STREET, OFF HIGH STREET.

DI MAGGIO'S PIZZERIA
61 Ruthven Lane

TEL: 334 8560

MON - THURS 12 NOON - 2.30PM
FRI/SAT 5PM - 12 MIDNIGHT
SUN 5PM - 12 MIDNIGHT

This Italian Pizzeria is of course dedicated to the great Italian Baseball slugger "Joking Joe". It is hardly surprising that the food served includes some of "joking joe's" favourites. Seafood, pasta, steaks and a choice of 21 different Pizzas including the special Pizza Jimmy. The "Jimmy" features crisp bacon, egg & baked beans.

Vegetarian Pizzas are excellent, fresh salads are an added attraction and the sweets are both extravagant and delicious.

Unusually, this friendly eating house welcomes children. High chairs are available for ankle biters and Di Maggio's caters to Children's birthday parties. 30 children could happily holler their way through mini portions & ladles of ice cream & jelly!

On Tuesdays an expert in "close up magic" or slight of hand, moves quietly between tables, dressed in black suit and bow tie. He performs card and scarf tricks which always delight the customers. The climax of his act involves firing a playing card up onto the ceiling, where it remains. This explains the cards stuck over the deep wine red ceiling.

A jazz trio plays on the small stage area from Sundays to Thursdays and although the rectangular room is quite small, the volume is never overpowering.

Normally there is a hum of friendly conversation encouraged by a warm & informal atmosphere. Staff are friendly & helpful.

Framed photos of the great movie stars cover the walls, Mitchum, Eastwood and of course Joe Di Maggio's wife Marilyn Monroe. American & continental bottled and canned beers are served pleasantly chilled.

THE SPAGHETTI FACTORY
30 Gibson Street

TEL: 334 2665

MON - THURS 12 NOON - 2.30PM 5PM - 12 MIDNIGHT;
FRI 12 NOON - 2.30PM ;5PM - 1AM
SAT 12 NOON - 1AM;
SUN 5PM - 12 MIDNIGHT

Industrious spaghetti eaters unite at this restaurant to choose from three variations and a choice of tempting sauces. "Be Hungry" is the neon sign which greets diners and your eye will be quickly drawn to the stuffed lion, leading you to wonder where its next meal is coming from. Ours came from a menu which included Honey-Glazed Winglets (to get you off to a flying start). The mane courses range from Design-a-Pizza, interesting Pastas, Fish and Chicken with a French influence and the inescapable Burger!.

Lion sized portions, especially the sweets, fresh Strawberries (in season), "great balls of fire" and "fly me to dunoon" are not intended for the faint hearted, so share one with a friend!

The "spag fag" as it is known to regulars has been a consistent favourite for ten years, attracting a wide range of clientele, catering for children (who get free meals on Saturdays) and west-end students.

Sunday night is theme night, when you get a free glass of wine with your meal, and if you happen to be attired in accordance with the advertised theme of the night, you'll be presented with a half litre of wine for your efforts. Very busy on Friday/ Saturday, but the staff manage to serve everyone without any noticeable problem.

GLASGOW'S BRIDGE OF SIGHS LEADING FROM CATHEDERAL SQUARE TO THE NECROPOLIS WAS BUILT IN 1832.

UBIQUITOUS CHIP
12 Ashton Lane

TEL: 334 5007

MON - SAT 12 NOON - 4.30PM; 5.30PM - 1.30AM

At its simplest, no restaurant guide of Glasgow would be complete without "the Chip". This is one of Glasgow's most famous restaurants and if you visit you will instantly see why. It is situated in Ashton Lane, off Byres Road, in the former courtyard of converted stables. The entire yard has been covered over with a transparent roof, which results in an airy, light environment. The floor is the original cobblestone and the walls, original brick. The most stunning feature however is the jungle-like effect of hundreds of tropical plants, trees, creepers and vines. A giant 35 foot monstera deliciosa reaches the roof and the far wall is totally covered in dense green ivy.

The total area is split into three sections. The main central courtyard can accommodate 40 diners, whilst a small raftered and vine covered terrace caters for another 15. A large inner, enclosed more traditional dining area is also featured. Reflecting the unusual nature of the building and decor, the food served is also different and very attractive. Starters include Laphroaig and Dill, marinated wild Salmon with Cream Cheese and Sybos, and Venison, Haggis and Neeps. Venison, Aberdeen Angus Steaks and Scottish Seafood are specialities as is the extensive range of Scottish Cheese.

If you like a wide selection of wines to choose from then you will be well pleased with the range and quality on offer. Rare and very much appreciated is the abundance of knowledgeable (some expert) staff on hand. The walls of the inner sanctum are adorned by the certificates of formal wine education undertaken by staff.

Prices are comparatively high, even for the west-end, but justifiable considering the quality and variety being provided. Diners tend to "dress" for a meal in the Chip and they usually linger for hours. A great deal of port is consumed and cigars are always in evidence.

Should you wish to wine and dine in an unusual and relaxed environment and you have the money to spend, savour the Chip.

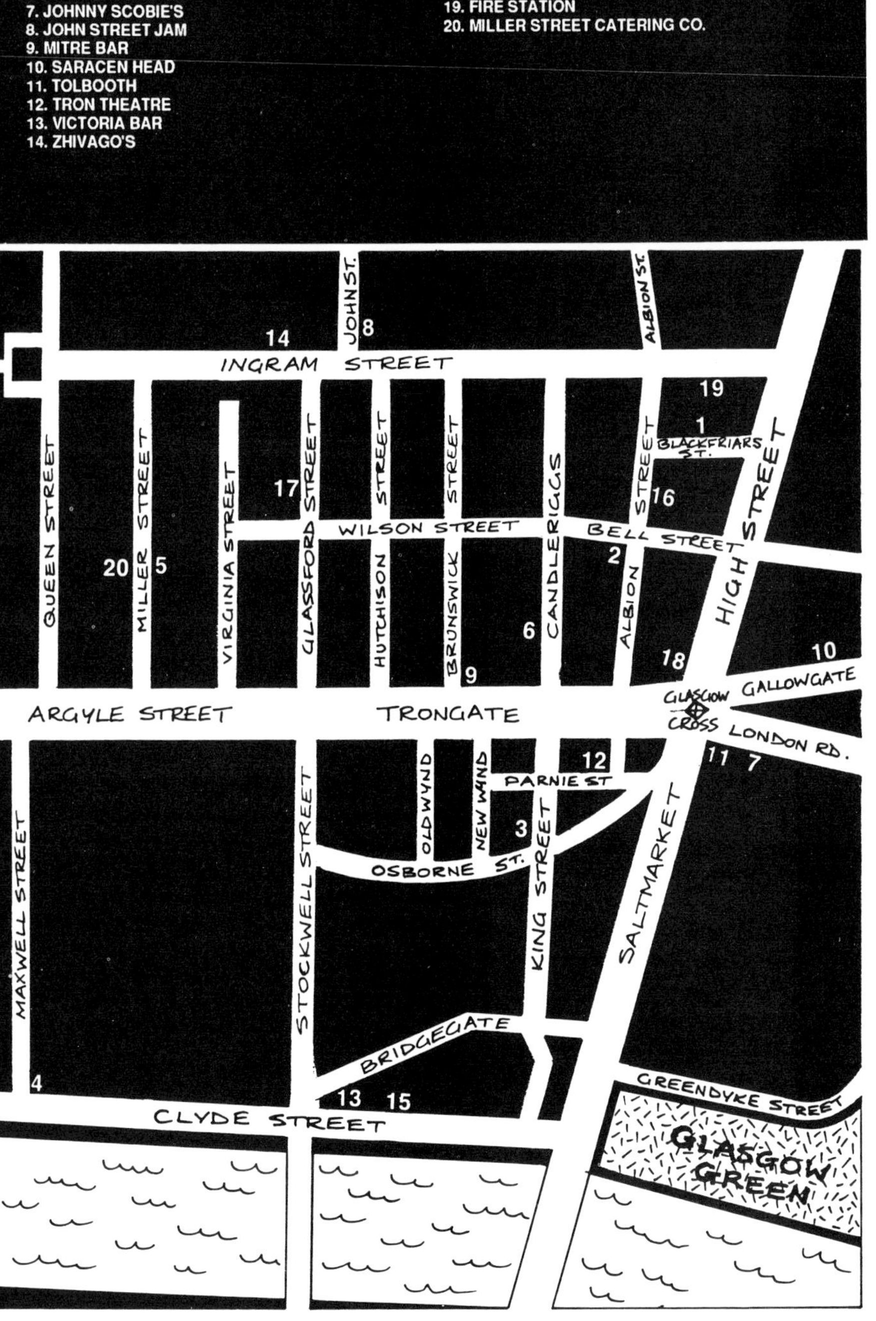

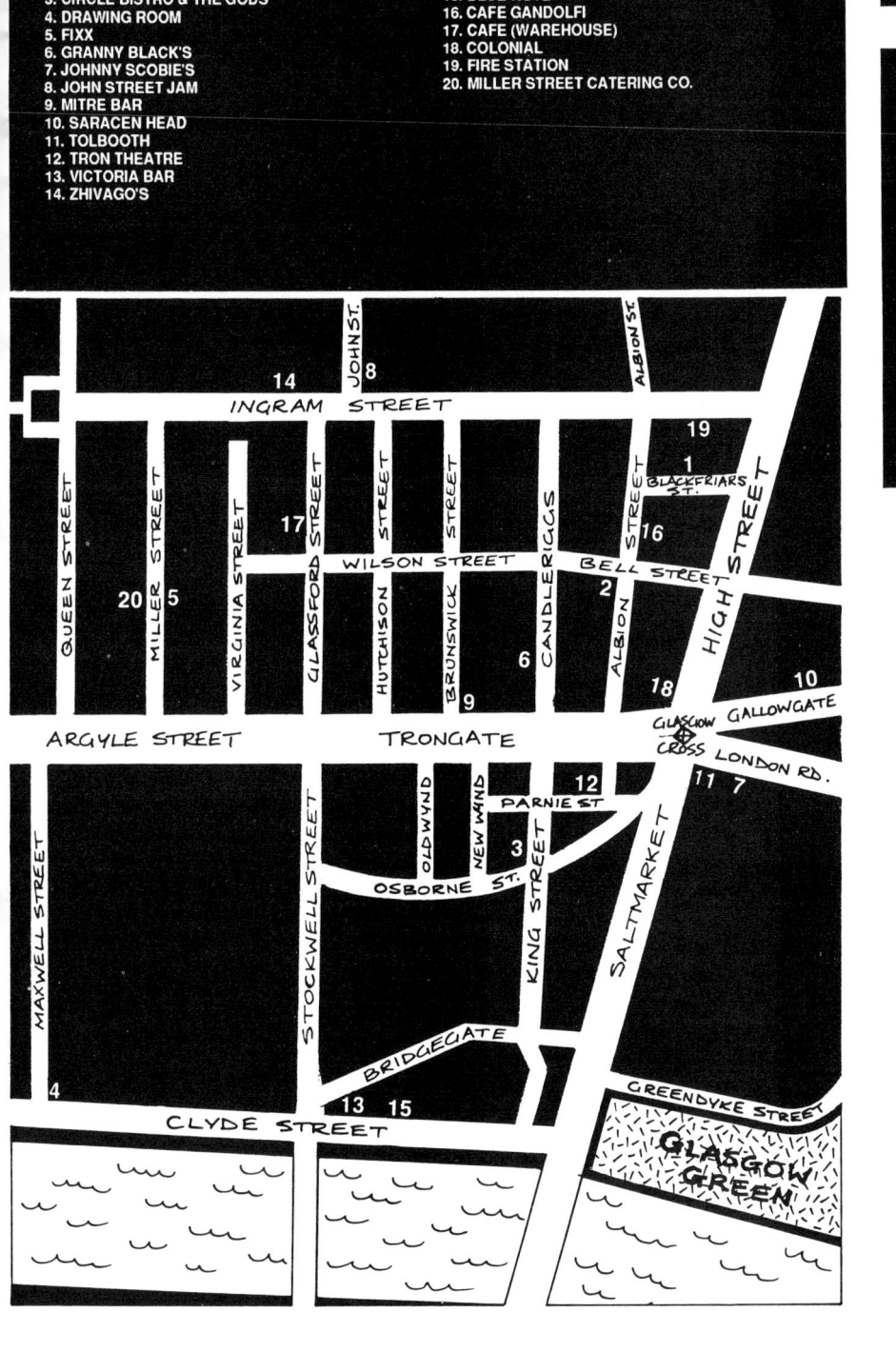

RESTAURANT GUIDE

MISS KATE CRANSTON RAN THE MOST POPULAR RESTAURANT IN THE 1901 EXHIBITION IN KELVIN PARK.

BLUE NOTE
72 Clyde Street

TEL: 552 6027

MON - FRI 9AM - 12 MIDNIGHT
SUNDAY 12.30 - 11PM

On two floors, the owners have tastefully refurbished this Merchant City restaurant/cafe/bar. Opened in August '86 when the Bridgegate Fish Market was transformed into an exclusive shopping centre housing hand knitted jumper shops and the like. The bar overspills into the shopping centre with glass topped tables and greenery, creating a very continental atmosphere. Already the Blue Note has established itself as host to up & coming new Glasgow bands such as

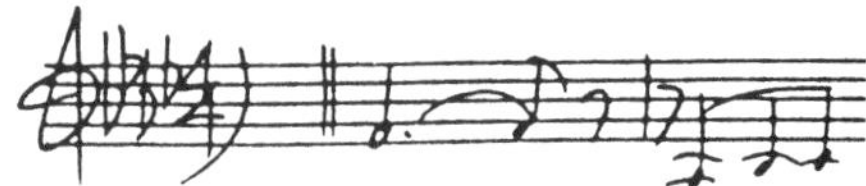

Deacon Blue. They also have regular live sets of Jazz and Folk music of an evening.

You can quite easily watch your meal being cooked in the open plan kitchen behind the bar. Specialities include Seafood and German dishes which are all reasonably priced, although it's likely to burn a hole in your pocket at lunchtimes, when you expect to pay less! Becks beer on draught, bottled Grolsch, San Miguel and a good range of house wines are on offer. Candlelit tables and dim lighting in the evenings create a relaxed but special atmosphere.

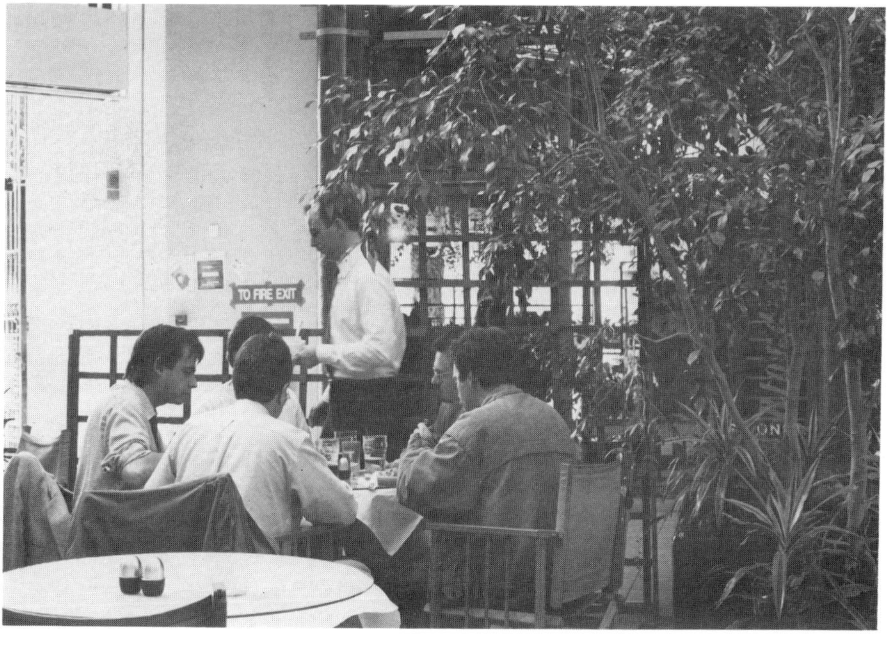

CAFE GANDOLFI
64 Albion Street

TEL: 552 6813

MON - SAT 9AM - 11.30PM

No matter the time of day or evening, the Cafe Gandolfi is always (quietly) busy, proving that this popular bistro/diner has lost none of its attraction since it first opened in 1982.

It was the first establishment offering a cosmopolitan menu to venture into the oldest part of Glasgow, but their confidence has proven to be justified as others have followed their example since.

The decor itself has an interesting history with the wood panelling originating from the state rooms of liners from days gone by and the revolving doors a small reminder of the magnificent St Enoch's Hotel, which is now buried below the Scottish Exhibition and Conference Centre.

You'll find a mixture of students & business people of all ages co-exist quite happily as customers of the cafe and the reasonable prices undoubtedly keep the cafe within the reach of most people.

The breakfast menu is continental, Gravadlax with Dill and Mustard sauce being the most expensive dish.

CAFÉ GANDOLFI

Yes, you may have spotted one potential difficulty: if your command of French is less than basic you might struggle to understand the menu, although the main dishes are also explained in English.

An excellent choice overall and good value for money. You will enjoy studying the decor, particularly the stained glass, wonderfully individual chairs and the bits and pieces of paraphernelia, including the antique camera. This is very appropriate as the cafe is named after a famous 19th Century camera-maker!

THE UBIQUITOUS CHIP BUILDING WAS A STABLE IN VICTORIAN TIMES.THE ORIGINAL COBBLED FLOOR IS RETAINED

THE CAFE (Warehouse)
61-65 Glassford Street

TEL: 552 4181

MON - SAT 10AM - 6PM

Located within "The Ware house", the building was designed and built in 1908 by the architectural firm of Dobbie & Robertson who have created an Art Nouveau clothing Warehouse. Found on the fourth floor, the Cafe is an unusual eating house.
A clean fresh leisurely atmosphere prevails, encouraging patrons to dally with the daily papers. The menu details a healthy range of french food, bagels, deep fried brie, stuffed croissants and croque monsieur, and the main courses are reasonably priced. If you like sweets, try the Apple and Banana Crumble! There are four types of coffee and five varieties of tea or a limited range of wines and bottled beers to choose from. The cafe is enjoyed by the young and old who wear up to the minute cote hauteur, much of which has probably been bought at the Warehouse! Plain, sunny, fresh decoration, with lots of natural daylight emphasises the light airy atmosphere; you are bound to feel relaxed and refreshed after eating here. There is always a penalty paid in such establishments, namely, you will have to queue at lunchtimes! The other bad news - it is only open 10am to 6pm, Mondays to Saturdays.

BRECHINS BAR IN GOVAN HAS A STATUE OF A CAT WITH A RAT IN ITS MOUTH, SAID TO BE THE FINEST "RATTER" IN GOVAN.

COLONIAL
25 High Street

TEL: 552 1923

MON - FRI 12- 2.30PM
TUES - SAT 6 - 10.30PM
CLOSED MONDAY EVENING AND
ALL DAY SUNDAY

The Colonial, owned by Peter Jackson, celebrated Chef, has been situated at the southern end of High Street since 1968. Offering an enticing menu which changes every month, it is one of all too few restaurants specialising in modern Scottish Fayre. The Colonial is to be found between the City Bakeries

and an art shop, but don't be fooled by its everyday surroundings. Being only a stones throw away from the city's fish market enables them to guarantee not only freshness but also variety in their seafood dishes. If you like to be a little adventurous with your food, take up the option of "menu surprise". The cook will surprise you with a special meal, which comes in at £19.45. Dishes recommended by the chef include Shellfish Bisque with Chives and Lemons, and Shallow Fried Turbot with Sesame Seeds and a Salmon Caviar Sauce.

The next surprise comes in the choice of wines and other beverages. With 150 wines and 50 half bottles to select from, it is said to offer one of the best wine lists outside London. A very respectable house wine would suit most palates, but the most discerning will delight in a bottle of 1928 Chateau Ausonne, a cheeky little claret available for only £175 (per bottle).

By now you might be thinking the Colonial is perhaps beyond the means of most. Let me redress the balance. For a really special occasion you'll get better value for money at the Colonial than in other less well established restaurants, and should you want to buy someone an impressive lunch, the executive lunch menu offers excellent value for money.

Booking is advised at weekends and the Colonial caters for private functions, but with a maximum capacity of 45, it is never loud, crowded or impersonal. The decor is demure and wouldn't compete with recently converted historical buildings which now house Glasgow restaurants. But then the Colonial has flourished in the unlikeliest venue for the past 20 years - quality is the key to its long standing success.

THE GLASGOW

42 YEARS AGO GLASGOW RESTAURANTS SERVED SHEEPS HEID AND PIGS TROTTERS ON WEDNESDAY WHICH WAS MARKET DAY.

FIRE STATION
33 Ingram Street

TEL: 552 2929

MON -THURS 12 -2.30PM;
5-11.30PM;
FRI 12-2.30PM;5-12.30PM;
SAT 12-1.00AM;SUN 12-11.30PM

As the menu itself states, customers are as likely to ask "was this really a fire station?" as they are "what is the soup of the day?". The restaurant itself only opened in November '87, however there has been a fire station in Ingram Street since 1900. The restaurant has kept the original layout of the station engine room including the splendid grecian marble walls which apparently came to the fire station as surplus from the City Chambers. One of the most famous firemen to serve in the Ingram Street brigade was "Wallace", who as far as our records tell us was the only canine employee of the fire brigade. For ten years they paid his licence and Wallace repaid them by running alongside the wagons protecting the horses from the local dogs who were in the habit of nipping their ankles. After his death in 1904, Wallace was stuffed and remained in the fire station until its closure in 1984. Current whereabouts unknown. The menu has a strong emphasis on pasta, using classic Italian recipes e.g., Lasagne and Carbonara etc and some original sauces e.g., Tagiatelle Rangoon - lighly curried chicken finished with a cream and mango sauce, as well as several vegetarian dishes. A full bar is available and draught beer is served by the glass or by the jug. Often in the evenings or at weekends you will find yourself being entertained by the resident pianist. The fresh food is a feast to the eyes and a selection of sumptuous puddings are hard to resist. No-one will pressure you to vacate your table, so sit awhile, and order the pudding later.

CLYDE-SIDE APPRENTICES' CONTRACTS SAID THAT MASTERS WERE TO GIVE THEM SALMON NO MORE THAN 3 TIMES A WEEK

MILLER STREET CATERING COMPANY
61 Miller Street

TEL: 226 5368

MON - FRI 8AM - 10PM
SAT 9AM - 10PM
SUN 9AM - 10PM

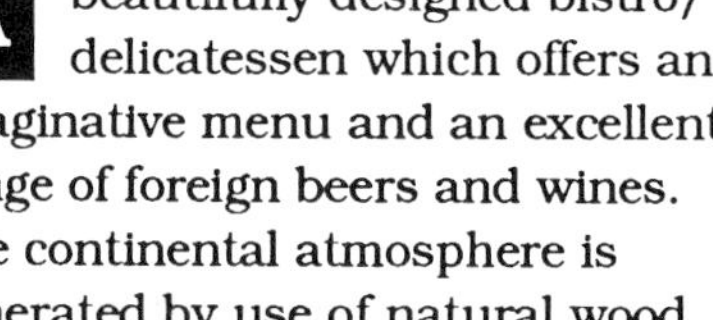

A beautifully designed bistro/ delicatessen which offers an imaginative menu and an excellent range of foreign beers and wines. The continental atmosphere is generated by use of natural wood and classic tiling together with the combined smells of fresh coffee and a range of food which will give you an appetite on arrival.

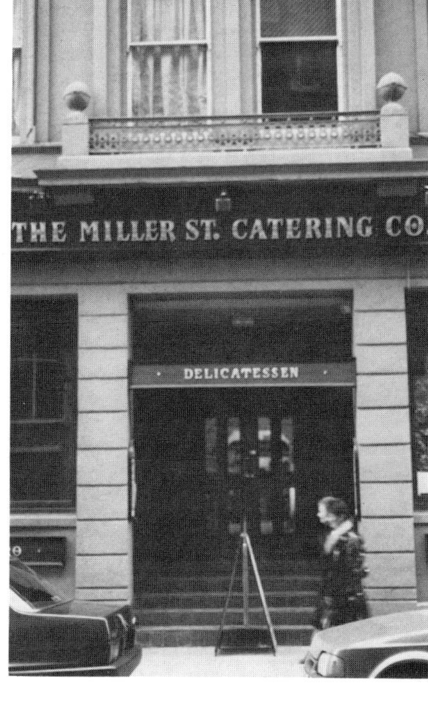

Once you've eaten here, you'll be tempted to make use of their integral delicatessen and "take home" some croissants, pate or cheeses. Whether you pop in for breakfast, elevenses or meet friends for lunch the quality of food and drink in this relaxed atmosphere will mean that you go back again and again for more of the same.

The menu includes Baked Brie with Provencal Sauce, Pastrami and Coleslaw on Rye, warm Mussel and Bacon Salads and delicious Stuffed Peppers. It comes as rather a surprise to find Baked Potatoes and Haggis on the same menu.

A similarly successful contradiction is found in the layout, with the Bistro, Delicatessen and Bar all definable areas which merge together conforming with the comfortable mood of the place.

1. FINLAY'S
2. FLORIDA PARK
3. GRANARY
4. JEANIE
5. J.J. BOOTH'S
6. MAXWELL'S
7. MISSION
8. MULBERRY HOTEL
9. NAPOLEONS
10. OLD SMIDDY
11. OUTHOUSE
12. VILLAGE

RESTAURANTS

13. DI MAGGIO'S
14. GREEK GOLDEN KEBAB
15. MEHFIL

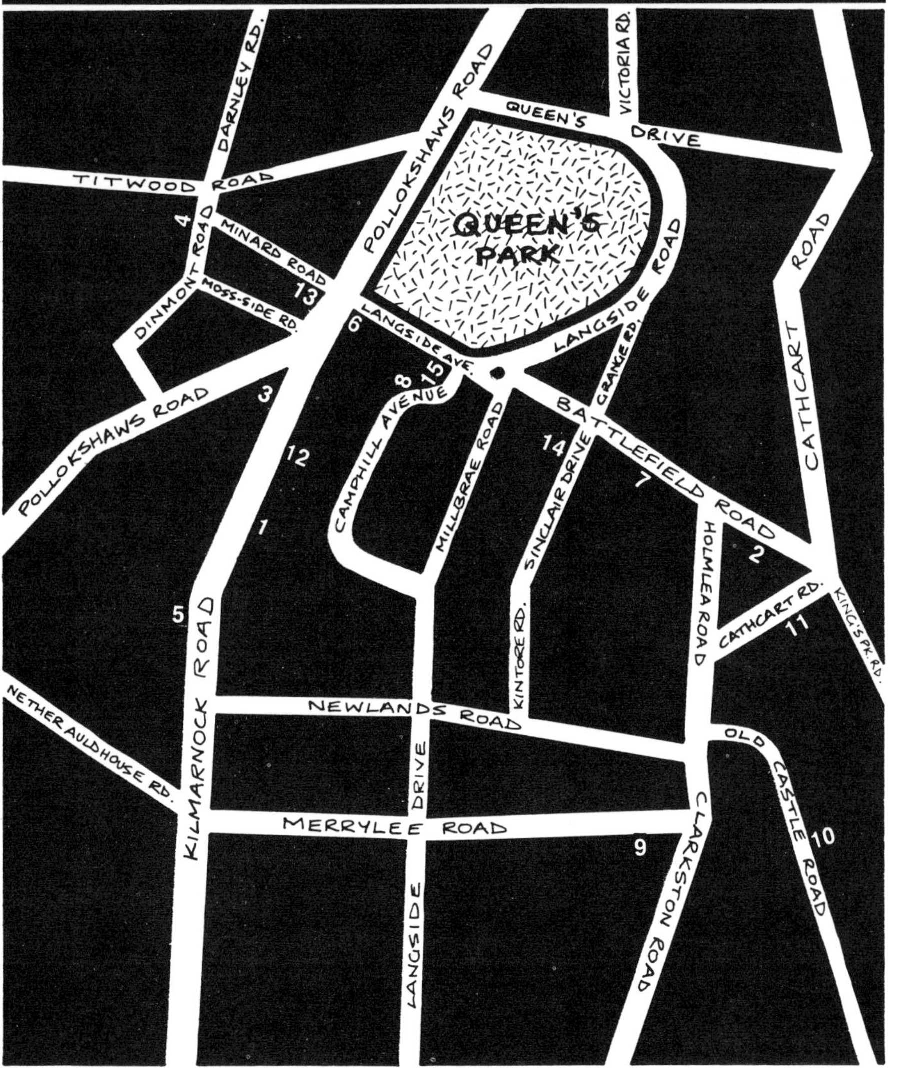

RESTAURANT GUIDE

A 'HALF & A HALF' WAS INVENTED BY AN IRISHMAN IN GLASGOW IN THE 18TH C. USING SMALL GLASSES FOR WHISKY AND BEER.

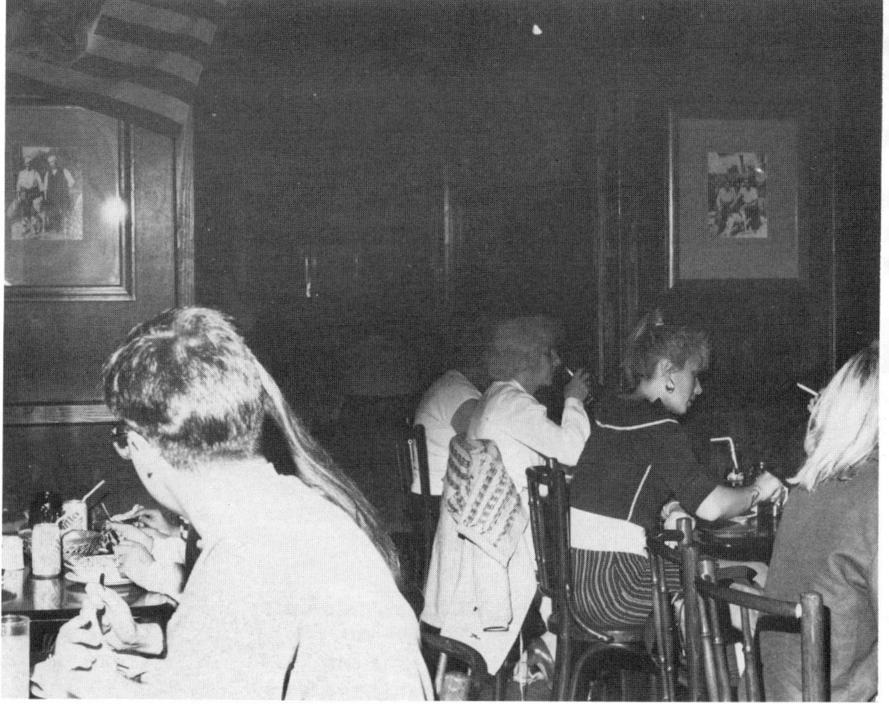

DI MAGGIO'S PIZZERIA
1038 Pollokshaws Road

TEL: 632 4194

MON - THURS 12 NOON - 11.30PM
FRI/SAT 5PM - 12 MIDNIGHT
SUN 5PM - 12 MIDNIGHT

Named after the famous Ameri can baseball player Joe Di Maggio, this pizzeria in the south side with another in the west end has set new standards of quality food and surroundings. Better than your average Pizza Hut or Pizzaland, the menu allows you to choose from any combination from a variety of toppings, anchovies, olives, tuna, assorted seafood etc. Also on offer are fresh pasta dishes such as Funghi E Prosciutto and the Di Maggio special recipe. A variety of tempting desserts are worth leaving a space for. Draught beer and house wines are inexpensive.

Whether its a candlelit dinner for two or an evening out for all the family, Di Maggio's is for you. However if you prefer to stay in and watch your favourite soap or T.V. programme, then a door to door delivery service is on offer to local residents.

GREEK GOLDEN KEBAB
34 Sinclair Drive

TEL: 649 7581

7 DAYS A WEEK
THURS - SAT 12 - 3PM
THURS - SUN 5PM - 2AM

This real authentic Greek Taverna, which has over the years built up a reputation as one of Glasgow's most atmospheric restaurants, is famous for it's "Tutti Frutti" scenes with Mr Clockerty and Suzie Kettles.

It is currently running on this reputation, and is running out of time. Complacency, high prices and oven chips were found as was City Bakeries Apple Pie barely heated up in the microwave.

I remembered with affection its cheap wood panelling, shiny wallpaper and plastic vines; these remained but this time accompanied by a Liverpudlian waitress, replacing that wonderful Greek man who taught me to dance.

Maria Kyriacou's specialities included Feta Salad, Tavva, Lamb with rice, cumin, spices, tomatoes, onions & black peppers. The ever popular Stifado, beef cooked with onions, spices, & wine is also on offer. The star attraction has to be Meze, where for a fixed price you choose the wine and Maria does the rest, providing a selection of hot & cold Greek meals. A comprehensive European menu is also available.

If you're feeling nostalgic for that Greek package holiday atmosphere, then this compact restaurant seating 24 is for you, but remember it costs alotta, lotta money!

MEHFIL RESTAURANT
2 Camphill Avenue

TEL: 636 1000

7 DAYS 12 NOON - 2PM;
5PM - 12 MIDNIGHT

Attached to the Mulberry Hotel the Mehfil is a popular Indian restaurant with locals. Across from Queen's Park the owners have tried, with some success, to create an equally fresh, airy atmosphere. Green, bold leafy prints line one wall whilst subtle pastel shaded walls and mirrors tastefully emphasise the relaxed aura in this compact eating house. There is very little natural light, and the evening lighting is also dim - perhaps this explains why it is a popular venue for romantically inclined couples?

The menu has all of the old favourites including some Punjabi Mehfil specialities, many requiring 24 hours notice, for example Mugham Masalam or the Mehfil Special Channa Chat. There are 15 speciality dishes to choose from and a European menu for those not dedicated to Indian cuisine. A very reasonable 3 course Business Lunch is offered, again with a choice of Indian or European dishes. A friendly restaurant which contributes to the culinary options open to south-siders.